Limited to Everyone

Limited
to Everyone

*An Invitation
to Christian Faith*

Robert Jones

THE SEABURY PRESS · NEW YORK

1982
The Seabury Press
815 Second Avenue
New York, N.Y. 10017

Library of Congress Cataloging in Publication Data
Jones, Robert, 1934 July 29-
    Limited to everyone.

        1. Apologetics—20th century.   I. Title.
BT1102.J66   201   82-5458
ISBN 0-8164-2381-4 (pbk.)   AACR2

Dedicated to the memory of Emile Cailliet,
late professor at Princeton Theological Seminary,
who told us over and over about
"the seamless robe of truth in the
God-bathed landscape of reality."

Contents

Preface

In the twenty-three years I've been a parish minister, I've dealt with hundreds of people who suffer from a bad reaction to the Christian faith. They say things like, "I was raised a Catholic, but then I went to college and it just didn't make sense anymore." Or, "My father was a staunch Presbyterian; we couldn't even read the funny papers on Sunday, but I can't raise my kids like that." Or, "I simply can't believe all those stories they told us in Sunday school now that I'm no longer eight years old." If you find yourself among these folks, I invite you to take a fresh look at Christianity. It isn't good that we should live our religious lives in terms of a bad reaction.

This book is for honest seekers, inquirers, and the curious, those who sense there may be something to the Christian way, but have little knowledge or experience of it. And it is for pastors and teachers to give to those who come seeking.

My experience tells me there must be thousands of people in every locality who are cut off from the church because of inadequate understandings which are no fault of their own. Their Christian training just didn't "take," or they didn't have any in the first place. Over the years they have picked up bits and pieces, just enough to be able to say, "I might be able to be a Christian if . . .," and then the stumbling block comes forth. "If I didn't have to believe that Jesus walked on the water or Jonah was swallowed by a whale."

Or, "If I could understand how God can be *up* there in heaven someplace when we know the universe is vast and curved and maybe shaped like a saddle." Or, "If the church weren't so rigid in its ways." I try to tell such folks that those same stumbling blocks bother *me*. This book shows how I try to deal with them. There is no reason a stumbling block has to keep us from the faith.

If you seek greater depth for your life, if you have snooped around churches in your search, if you are trying to make your way with a third-grade understanding of Christianity and an adult-level mastery of everything else, if your training for your occupation has outstripped your education in theology by many years, this book is written for you. If you are stuck at certain passages of the Bible but have not found a way to interpret it as a whole, this book may be of help. If you feel an uncomfortable gap between what you know and understand about life and what you know and understand about faith, I was thinking about you as I wrote. The book attempts to narrow some of those gaps, but in the attempt, it takes the gaps seriously. If you are one who feels down deep that the tug of life and the pull of faith need not be in opposite directions, I hope you will accept this invitation to look at Christianity in a candid way.

I have written out of my own struggle with the Christian faith. It is not an exhaustive study, but a serious attempt to make sense of God, life, the church, and the universe in terms of our present day and age. I deal with questions that have bothered me as I have sought to find my own way. I have tried to overcome Christianity's traditional sense of superiority and exclusiveness. I have worked hard to find an approach to the Bible which doesn't make light of it but at the same time does not embarrass my contemporary understanding of life and the world. I have fought the battle of heart versus head, seeking a faith that is intellectually satisfying and at the same time warming to the soul. I am convinced such a faith can be found. For me, it is the only kind worth finding. I have set down the way I go about my quest in the hope that it will be of use to others who are seeking their way.

To my mind, a relevant and satisfying faith requires hard thinking, a number of stories, a bit of the personal touch, a measure of openness, and a dash or two of humor. I hope I have gotten them in about the right proportions.

Robert Jones
Guerneville, California
January 20, 1982

Limited to Everyone

How forceful are honest words!
Job 6:25

· 1 ·

The Christian God
Is Too Exclusive

"Tell me, what do you *really* think about God?" The question comes up at the punch bowl after the wedding, in the locker room of the tennis club, at the mailbox or the bus stop, at any number of places where people know who I am or what I do for a living. Somehow, because I'm a minister, it is assumed that I would rather talk about God than the weather or almost anything. Though that's not always true, I try to accommodate such folks, because I do believe that talking about God can be important and maybe even good for us as well.

What do you *really* think about God? With the accent on the *really,* as it often is, the question is more than a casual request for my opinion. There's a little dig in it some place. It implies that what I *really* think about God may be different from my official position or from the orthodox statements of the church. There is a measure of truth in that. It is a truth that everyone who struggles with faith questions knows. Official positions and what we really think are not always the same. It has been my purpose and privilege over the years to tell people that's all right. God honors honesty as well as orthodoxy. God is not contained in the doctrines. Doctrines are the summaries of the experience of the church over the centuries, and they are worth knowing about. But we all have our own thoughts, and they are worth looking at and sharing.

What do I *really* think about God? I, a Christian, an ordained minister of the church, a seeker after truth, and a struggler with the faith, really think that the Christian God is too exclusive. It's not that God is exclusive, but we tend to conceive of God in exclusive terms. Christians aren't alone in this, but we are prominent. We tend to assume that believing in God rules some people in and some people out. I wonder. I wonder if the great God of the universe relates differently to different people on the basis of what they believe. I realize this may border on heresy, but I can't help it. I wonder.

Christian history is an embarrassment of exclusiveness. The Crusades, the Inquisition, the continuous animosity between one group and another, are blots on the record. There seems to be embedded deep in the human soul a propensity to keep others out. We like to think we know the ones God has chosen for blessing and the ones chosen for the eternal burn. We are, I suppose, so insecure about our status in this life that we spend a lot of time figuring out ways to disqualify our friends and neighbors from the next. As I recall, not even Jesus speculated on this subject. When asked who was in and who was out of the heavenly kingdom, he replied, in effect, "Only God knows about those things." Far be it from us, then, to presume to know whom God has chosen for this or that everlasting future.

I am afraid we still have notions of God as a territorial deity. We assume God watches over us and our kind in order to protect us from them and their kind. We have a little dog at home who isn't much good for anything except that my daughter loves her dearly, and she will bark like crazy when anyone even gets close to setting a foot on our property. Too often we think of God like that. God is the one who watches at the boundaries of our lives, keeping away those ideas, influences, and people who might challenge or change us. Yes, the Christian God is too exclusive, and that bothers and embarrasses me. Furthermore, too few of us are battling against the idea of an exclusive God.

A preacher can get into a lot of trouble trying to fight that battle.

Some of our best church folks have a terrible time believing that God might love, or at least like a little bit, those awful heathens, the greedy Moslems, the dreamy Hindus, the libertine atheists, the godless communists, or even those clannish Jews—whose Bible and heritage we share so intimately. The theory has been that God loves these other people in a general sort of way, for after all, "God loves everybody," but in order to have God's important love, in order to know God's "saving" grace and mercy, these people have to become Christians. I wonder. I realize that to wonder at this point calls into question the greater part of the church's missionary enterprise. I'm not sure I want to give up all those marvelous missionary stories I've heard and told, but I am convinced we have to give up the sense of Christian superiority that often lies behind those stories. If we really believe in one, true, living God, then we must affirm the validity of other religions and cultures. I don't see any way around that.

I wonder if we have ever taken seriously the notion of one, true, living God. It is clear to me that if there is one, true, living God, then we don't have to worry too much about how other people perceive God. Sure, some perceptions of God are better than others, more helpful, more conducive to health, wholeness, justice, and peace—and some perceptions of God can be downright damaging—but I don't see where the Christians have exclusive ownership of the helpful and healthful perceptions of God. No, our view of God has caused its share of the holy wars. To believe in one, true, living God is to struggle with the inclusiveness of that belief.

If there is one, true, living God, then all things, all beings, all creatures, all hearts, all souls, all minds, and all bodies, are related to God in a positive way. If there is one, true, living God, then everything and everyone knows something of God's everlasting and unbounded love. If there is one, true, living God, then nothing in a holy book can be interpreted so as to rule some people out. If there is one, true, living God, then there is never any justification for bringing harm to someone in the name of God. If there is one, true, living God, then by that fact alone, we are all brothers and sisters, and we are bound to the rocks and stars, the liquids and gases, and everything that creeps or crawls or gallops or swims. I wonder if we have even begun to fathom the fantastic implications which flow so naturally out of monotheism.

So, it's not just the exclusiveness of various Christian groups I'm talking about, not just the traditional lack of charity among the Christian traditions and denominations. It's not just the kind of thing Halfred E. Luccock is getting at when he tells of a traveling tent preacher who came into a frontier community and proclaimed, "The main trouble with this town is whiskey and the Methodists." It's not even that we still have trouble getting the races together in church, or the young and the old, or the singles and the marrieds, embarrassing as all of that is. No, the deep down exclusiveness of the Christian concept of God is that it leaves the universe out. We have such a people-centered way of faith that we leave out huge chunks of reality when we try to think about God. The church, today, exists "to meet the religious needs of the people." Our theology centers on the meaning of being a person. This is a noble enterprise, but I am becoming convinced that the full meaning of personhood will not emerge until we get beyond strictly personal concepts in our talk about life and God and the universe. There is a whole galaxy full of spinning reality out there. Numberless galaxies beyond that. Surely those great globs of matter and the processes which seem to control them have to be taken into account. We have claimed for faith the province of Sigmund Freud. That's all to the good. Now we must grapple with the world of Carl Sagan.

The idea of a personal God should never suggest to us that God is personal in ways which are limited by our understanding of what a person is. The Bible begins with a picture of God at work, speaking and creating all that is. "In the beginning, God . . .," it says. Let that notion rattle around in our heads for a while, and we have to let go of some of our barriers against seeing value in all lives, all cultures, all seekings for the truth. If the Bible ended right there after just four words, we would have plenty to meditate upon for a lifetime. My meditations cause me to think that the processes and phenomena which comprise our lives exist in God. My life and its entire context move and breathe and have their meaning in that "larger" context, which is supreme, infinite, and divine. This great God of the universe may not be personal in the way I understand personhood, but I sense, at times, a cosmic friendliness, concern, and love directed toward me. I sense this most profoundly when I feel it directed also toward every life, every person, every thing. If there is one, true, living God, then all those spinning worlds out there, and everyone that might be in them, are included in grace and love and glory.

· 2 ·

Proof

Another question that often comes up is, "Can you prove to me there is a God?" The answer, in a word, is no. But that's not the whole story. There are several "proofs" for the existence of God which have been around for a long time. Most of them are not really proofs, however, but arguments, often thoughtful arguments, which give reasons for faith in God. Without faith, it is questionable if the arguments would work. And yet it is good to think about these things. Too often the churches have said to people, "Check your minds at the door." Too often being a person of faith has meant holding on to ridiculous notions about life and the universe. Hegel, the philosopher, said in effect, "Faith is philosophy for those with low IQ's." One task of the church is to try to prove him wrong.

Theology, over the centuries, has been the attempt to present the God of the Bible in ways that are relevant and sensible to the prevailing nonbiblical world view. Thus, the ideas of Plato lie behind the theology of the great fourth-century Christian thinker St. Augustine, and the work of Aristotle was a model for St. Thomas Aquinas whose theology, though written in the thirteenth century, still stands very tall in Christian thought. This pattern has continued. The dominant theologians of the early twentieth century often worked against a background of European existentialism. They were interested in the experiences of loneliness and anxiety in our industrialized and war-torn world. God was perceived as one who called us together and saved us either by giving the gift of inner courage or by speaking a word from beyond the anxiety-producing situation. Names like Barth, Brunner, Tillich, and Niebuhr were prominent. Their influence is still very great.

A trouble these days, however, is that there is no agreed-upon dominant philosophy. Therefore, theology has tended to go this way and that. Theology books are likely to be as much about literature or politics or sociology as they are about God. There is the theology of liberation, theology of the environment, theology of the arts. There is narrative theology, biography as theology, and various forms of groupiness as theology. There are theologies for sex, theologies for jogging, theologies for playing golf, and theologies for fixing motorcycles. There are theologies about almost everything except the struggle to believe in God. I sometimes don't know what to think about all of this.

But at other times I do, or at least I think I do. Sometimes I wake up early, and in the dim, quiet light of early dawn I see a thought to follow like a path through a wood. I will suddenly remember a book or a lecture or some idea or phrase that seems to point a way. One phrase from years ago still comes back to me. "It is more important to love God than to believe in God, but even more important than that is to try to do both." I still try to do both, to love God and believe in God at the same time. I want both concepts and feelings in my faith, ideas and mysteries, thoughts and experiences. I'm not sure I would want to prove the existence of God apart from faith, but my kind of faith needs to be aware of the available proofs.

Most commonly, the existence of God is argued on the basis of the beauties and structures of nature. God uses this argument on Job toward the end of that remarkable Old Testament story. After Job has suffered through pus and boils and the horrible advice of his three friends, God tells him to look up at the heavens and see how well everything is arranged. The sun and moon and stars shine in their places, all the heavenly bodies are where they belong. And

God tells him to look around and notice the amazing ways the different animals reproduce themselves. Eagles hatch eggs, lions give birth to live cubs, the insects do what they do, and all of that. "Who could have devised this and set it all in motion save the Lord God of heaven and earth?" God asks.

"That's just what I've been saying all along," Job replies.

"I know," says God, "and you have been faithful beyond what anyone could ask." Soon after this conversation, Job's fortunes are restored. The argument from nature sees him through. It is a beautiful argument beautifully received.

This argument often lends itself to beauty. I once heard a preacher describe the human eye. He had gone to a lot of trouble to tell about the intricacies to be found there. Finally he said, "And there you have it, thousands upon thousands of tiny rods and cones working together in their incomprehensibly complex ways so that you and I can be overwhelmed by a sunset. Only God could arrange anything as marvelous as that." Same old beautiful argument. It may not be a proof, but I'm glad we have it.

The argument from nature often moves toward the notion of the ultimate beginning or end of all things. We look upon the vastness of the universe and wonder, "What got all this started?" Or we tremble in our temporary lives and ask, "Where is all this headed?" God, it is argued, is causer and completer, alpha and omega, beginning and end. These arguments are part of a deep human desire for meaning. We look hard for causes and purposes. A sense of direction is precious to us, powerful and freeing. Another great argument for the existence of God is based on this widespread human need. Since humans everywhere seek for meaning, this argument goes, we must recognize the ultimate source and fulfillment of this search as God. "Our hearts are restless until they find their rest in thee," St. Augustine said. Modern preachers have spoken of the "God-shaped vacuum in every human soul." This argument was very important to me in my younger days when I was wondering what my life should be, what purpose I wanted to give myself to. To be truthful, it is still important for me. I want to think I have counted for something that has a chance to last. I don't see how that can happen unless my life is part of the life of the everlasting God.

A further argument for God is the one from morality or conscience. Even though there are different moralities, the reasoning here goes, still everywhere you look you find people who have a sense of right and wrong. This inner law is said to be put there by God. If nothing else, this argument lends itself to some helpful thinking about God as the foundation of ethical behavior. For sure, we need standards and structures, and most of the societies of the world have been held together by a belief in divinely ordained principles of conduct. God the lawgiver is an important theme. Can human behavior be a matter of divine concern? Are our actions with each other so crucial that God is involved in them? Such questions raise many daily decisions above a purely mundane level. It is probably good for us to feel that what we do has that kind of significance. From this argument we get a view of God as the weaver of the social fabric as well as the fashioner of the universe.

It is clear, I am sure, that these arguments do not establish God as an objective reality apart from faith. The arguments buttress faith, they do not create faith. Furthermore, the God these arguments point to can seem pretty aloof at times. "First Cause," it turns out, is a name given to the God who was said to be proved by the argument from causation. This God has been characterized as "the Great Watchmaker," who got everything ticking and then went off to more interesting pursuits. During the eighteenth century, this was a popular theological notion. Many of our nation's founding fathers adhered to it, Ben Franklin among them.

The God of the arguments is not the God of the Bible who moves and feels and speaks and bleeds. Here lies some tough work for theology. How do we understand this seemingly changeable biblical God and still have a notion of a consistent universe? Is the God of worship, prayer, song, and sacrament the same God I can believe in when I'm trying to think straight? The arguments for God may not be absolute proofs, but they help us grapple with questions such as these. A lot of us, I feel, are looking for a God we can believe in as well as worship. We may not be able to prove beyond all question that God exists, but we can discover reasons for faith by turning our minds upon the deepest longings of our hearts. I need to ponder causes. I need a sense of purpose. I need a focus for deciding what is right and wrong. Anything less than God seems too little for this. And I am often overwhelmed by the grandness of nature, the beauties of this world, the brevity and loveliness of life. Whom do I thank for it all? I thank God.

· 3 ·

The Wager

If someone were to say, "But none of those arguments really work; they go so far, then stop," I would agree. Sooner or later, when talking about God, our words must stop, our thoughts must give way, and we must wait in silence and awe for new words and thoughts that will also be found lacking. Different people, different theologians in fact, have different ways of "tuning into" the mystery of God. Some will feel that any hard, probing thought is inappropriate. For them God is so vast or so personal that only a deep, heartfelt, overwhelming response can relate us to God in adequate ways. Others seem to feel that our knowledge of God is faulty unless we refine the arguments, define the terms, and seek after greater and greater preciseness in our theological statements. My own pilgrimage embraces both approaches. I want to feel "strangely warmed" as Martin Luther felt one day when he was reading his New Testament, but I also want to question and probe and think and come as close to "proving" God as I can. My belief is that a satisfying faith requires the fullest possible response from both heart and mind. If I'm not mistaken, this is the legacy of the great monastics of the Christian way. There is thought and contemplation. There is prayer and silence. There is the overwhelmed soul. All are important. All are involved in knowing and loving God.

At the very least, we must recognize that ideas have their times. There is a history to concepts just as there is a history to anything else. Today, though we tend to think of God as personal, we usually turn our backs on older ideas about God as one huge person. When we talk about a "personal God" we usually mean that God is personally involved in our lives, in our marriages and divorces, our decisions and confusions, our revolutions and our yearnings for peace. The notion of a personal God seems to fly in the face of the impersonal character of so much in contemporary life. In the last few hundred years the search for truth has been drastically cut off from the idea of a personally involved God. The physical and social sciences seem to proceed without worrying about ultimate causes and final purposes. Many branches of knowledge seem to look to no point of reference beyond their own fields of study. A "big bang" got everything started. Chemical and electrical accidents produced life where there was no life. Right and wrong are the products of parental pressure and cultural conditioning. From many angles, we have a picture of humans alone in the universe, unless, of course, other accidents on other planets produced other creatures we have yet to meet. We have available to us a comprehensive world view based on naturalistic and humanistic premises. I am afraid we religionists have to admit that the arguments for this world view are at least as valid as the traditional arguments for the existence of God. If so, we had better make sure that our faith in God doesn't live or die in the arguments. We had better find a way to let God exist beyond the limits of our concepts, at least until our concepts grow and become more adequate.

The Bible, of course, does not set out to prove God. It assumes God. It opens with a picture of God at work—speaking, creating, arranging. The rest of the story shows God involved with the creation and its creatures. God visits them, leads them, seeks them, rescues them. God makes them whole. To do this, God chooses a particular family through whom a promise is given that all the world should be blessed. There is a specificness about all of this which the arguments don't capture. There is the sense of a divine personality. God is aware. God communicates. God desires to be related and is free to act on that desire. At a most crucial time in the story God uses the personal pronoun "I." It is part of God's name. Moses hears it and takes off his shoes and is never the same again.

The contrast between the God of the arguments and the God of the Bible was perceived in a most sensitive way by the seventeenth century mathematician, scientist, inventor, and mystic, Blaise Pascal. This brilliant Frenchman was part of a movement which put him at odds with the church of his day. His efforts laid the groundwork for much of our modern mathematics. He devised a calculator. He invented the syringe, for which he got into more trouble with the church, for in those days the church held to the dictum "Nature abhors a vacuum." Pascal's work in mathematics was abetted by visits to the gambling dens of Paris. He was fascinated by the odds in card games, and this fascination led to breathtaking insights into the calculus of probability. It also led to his famous argument for the existence of God based on the notion of wager.

Briefly put, the argument goes like this. If you bet there is a God, and there is a God, you win everything. If you bet there is a God, and there is no God, you lose nothing. If you bet there is no God, and there is a God, you lose everything. And if you bet there is no God, and there is no God, you lose nothing. Therefore, said Pascal, only a fool would bet there is no God, for that is the only position from which you can lose everything and have no chance to win anything. I have heard philosophy students say that the argument is airtight. It does not, of course, prove the existence of God, but it does give a nice twist to the options available.

Pascal himself was not limited by his argument. His faith was warm and close and real to him. He perceived "light" in his room one night and wrote about the experience very carefully, as would a scientist observing something surprising. "Fire, light, unspeakable joy," were the phrases he used. "Not the God of the philosophers, but the God of Abraham, Isaac, and Jacob, the God and Father of the Lord Jesus Christ." I tend to feel that no matter how thoroughly or unthoroughly we are convinced by the arguments for God, they will not help us very much until we have some kind of experience of God, not necessarily as dramatic as Pascal's, but something we sense as just as real.

The validity of "the wager" as an argument for God is that it gives a sense of what it feels like to believe. There is a thrill to having bet on an outcome which is beyond our control. Faith is like that. No matter how fully we have understood it, no matter how well we have it figured out, believing in God will always be thrilling. For belief does not capture God. Proofs, even if they work, do not cause God. Theology, as the attempt to understand faith, is part of the faith response. We enter in. We move with the flow. And we place our bets and thrill to the game as it unfolds. We are part of something awfully big. Betting on God helps us to feel enhanced rather than diminished. It gives us a chance to be related to reality at the core. I am one of those who is glad for such a chance.

Feelings and structures. Thoughts and passions. Belief and worship. Our minds tend to separate these avenues by which reality comes to us. We put them in contrast. We tear the universe apart in our attempt to understand it. We are at a time, perhaps just the beginning of a time, when it is being recognized that knowledge can unify as well as analyze. We are at a time when people in many contexts seem to be experiencing something of the "light." We are at a time when people of various religions are looking beyond the tight structures of their own traditions. Faith and reason may be moving closer together. Let's hope that they are.

· 4 ·

The Raw Material
of the Spiritual Life

When we mention Pascal's vision of the light, Luther's being strangely warmed, or any of a number of happenings including our own prayers or anxieties or hopes, we are getting close to the starting point of faith. Faith begins in experience. Faith arises from what goes on inside us and around us.

An experience is just that. My experience. What happens, what I cause to happen, and what I make of it. There are happenings no one has the right to interpret for me. No one has the right to tell me what my dreams mean, unless I ask them to. No one has the right to tell me what I *really* mean when I say, "I love you," or "I'm mad at you," or "I don't care one way or the other." I alone get to decide what those things mean to me. So it is with my experience of God. Theology can help me understand it. Biblical interpretation can be a source of images, stories, categories, and values by which my experience of God comes to me. Prayer and worship and serving others can be among the ways I experience God. But my experience of God is mine. I own it. It does not belong to the church or the tradition. It belongs to me.

I would guess that no two people experience God in exactly the same way. Too often, Christian theology has tried to limit people's experience of God rather than to help them understand it. It has been said, for instance, "Your experience of God is not valid unless you believe in the Trinity." But there are many understandings of the Trinity, none of which seems utterly complete. It has been said, "Your experience of God does not count unless you understand the two natures of Christ." But there are several theories about the two natures of Christ, each with strengths and weaknesses. It has been said, at certain times and places in the history of Christianity, that "Your experience of God is not acceptable unless it includes a rapturous spiritual upheaval." At other times and places it has been said, "Your experience of God is not valid if it does include a rapturous spiritual upheaval." I believe it is fruitless, even harmful, for the church to tamper too much with people's experience. An experience is an experience. It is just there in one's life and memory, like getting married, like giving birth, like being overwhelmed by a sunset. Experience is the raw material of the spiritual life. It is my guess that it is best to leave it more or less in its raw state until, through other experiences, through study and contemplation, through contact with others, through the mere passage of time, patterns of meaning begin to emerge.

I find that one of the best things I can do for people is to believe them when they tell me about an experience. Over the years, I've heard enough so that it takes quite a bit to really surprise or shock me. People have all sorts of experiences and many times they want to relate the most profound ones to God. Some people take great stock in their dreams as messages from God. Now I've read Freud and know what he said about dreams—that basically they are messages from our own unconscious selves. But for people who haven't read Freud, and even for some who have, God can still speak in dreams. Sometimes these people make important decisions on what comes to them in their sleep. So long as it fits into the rest of life, so long as the interpretation of the dream is flexible enough to allow for change, I find it often helps people get focused and motivated to relate their dreams to God. Furthermore, I have not noticed that people who make decisions this way are markedly less successful than those who figure and calculate and weigh alternatives. In fact, some people do both. I suppose most of us do, and it's probably a good thing.

These days, a lot of people are meditating. Much of the teaching and training for this comes out of the oriental religions. I have noticed a bit of irritation on the part of official Christianity about this. But people who meditate tell me they get everything from peace and quiet to overwhelming mystical experiences from meditating. They say they are better able to cope with daily frustrations. They claim they are nicer to husbands, wives, children, bosses, employees, customers, gripers, and fellow commuters because of their time of quiet. This is valid experience. Though in recent centuries it has been de-emphasized, there is a wealth of meditative resources in the Christian tradition. The church should try to recapture it.

I know some people who seem to interpret every coincidence as a sign of God's special intervention. I don't like this way of seeing things, because it makes God seem rather capricious. But I have learned to button my lip when I hear these things. If some people can see God's direct action in their getting a parking place, it means at the very least that they sense God in many of the details of life I just take for granted. The main thing about this is to refrain from forcing our experiences or our interpretations on other people. If you think God gets you parking places, that's fine. Just don't say my faith is inadequate if I don't see it that way. God never got me a parking place, but once God helped me sink a crucial putt.

Sadly, it happens that a certain kind of religious experience becomes the basis for inclusion in a Christian fellowship. Too often, churches are held together by orthodoxies of experience. There are the sawdust trail churches, the crisis resolution churches, the nurturing churches, the liturgical churches, the correct theology churches, the speaking in tongues churches, and, I'm sure, all kinds of other churches. We are divided over what makes a valid Christian experience. That, surely, is a sign of some holy wrongheadedness. We'll use most anything to rule people out.

I see people come into our services of worship with big black

Bibles in their hands. They are, obviously, visitors. Our people just don't carry Bibles to church, and that's all there is to that. But many other people do. Often the ones who do, when they visit us, are seen to frown, squirm, look up, look down, look away, and leave early. It makes me sad, not just because they give fresh evidence that there are times when I don't get through, but because I feel they are cutting themselves off from a chance to hear the name of their God uttered in a new way for them. But I do the same thing when I go to their kind of church. I fidget. I sigh. I may, Lord forbid, even shake my head. I'm not hearing any of my favorite phrases. I don't quite get the hymns or the way they are being sung. The prayers seem too chummy with the Almighty. So I resist. And I miss a chance to have my heart warmed by a different fire. I am having an experience that doesn't fit my structures, so I rule it out. Sad.

But if God is God, we don't have to worry about whether our experiences fit into some kind of structure. God is the ultimate structure and the ultimate freedom for all our experience. Our job is to try to find out what our experience means. Our experiences and their meaning exist in God. That is the safety we have. We learn of God and understand God in and through the experiences of our lives and our attempts to understand them.

The Bible is full of instances in which disasters, successes, battles, peace treaties, injustices, right judgments, sleepless nights, times of rest, scary dreams, beautiful visions, terminal illness, miraculous healing, birth, death, fishing trips, business trips, forced marches, strolls in the garden, imprisonment, breaking loose, loneliness, mail from home, sermons, summons, unusual weather, poverty, luxury, disappointment, getting what you want, and almost anything else you can name, become occasions for experiencing God. The Bible is full of such situations because life is. The Bible story is our story. It is also God's story. Our story and God's story become the same story as we experience our lives and try to understand what they mean.

· 5 ·

With the "Amen"
I Relaxed

"Have you ever had an experience of God?" people ask me. The way I define that question is that I have had lots of them. Sunsets, music, especially good jazz. The Van Gogh exhibit I saw in Kansas City. Some memorable dinners. Laughter. Any time I feel the huge sweep of life or the deep sorrow of the world or the great beauty of nature and art, at any number of times and in any number of places, I experience God. I don't think this makes me special or unusual. In fact, the way I see it, there is no reason not to experience God twenty-four hours a day. I myself have never been able to do that—not even for a day, not even for an hour—but that's my problem. God's presence in the world doesn't depend on my recognizing it. God's interest in my life doesn't stop when I no longer sense it. My experiences have their place and movement in God. That's a constant I count on. Just because my receiver is turned off doesn't mean the signal isn't there.

I might single out two experiences which have been especially important to me. The first occurred when I was about halfway through college. I had been having a hard time figuring out what I was going to do when I got out of school. I changed majors a few times—business, engineering, education—and finally took a poetry course which, to my great surprise, I found I truly loved. I had been raised to think of poetry as pretty much sissy stuff, but I became an English major and just ate it up. I'll never forget Professor Mark Shorer reading T. S. Eliot's "Journey of the Magi" to a packed auditorium in Dwinelle Hall in Berkeley. It was on the day before Christmas recess. Something must have been tugging the memory chords of many of us, for when he finished, we were all on our feet applauding. "The Wise Man story," I thought to myself, "I never thought I would clap for that." Not long afterward I began going to church again for the first time in years.

During this time a group of young men from Sacramento pledged our fraternity. They were Presbyterians, and I started going to church with them. One weekend, the Sacramento gang invited me home with them. We had a great time. One of the group played the banjo like a pro, and we spent a lot of time singing old ballads and drinking a lot of beer to go with the singing. On Sunday afternoon, Billy Graham was having a rally at the State Fair Grounds. As a lark, we decided to go. Presbyterians, after all, are way beyond that Graham stuff.

Graham preached his sermon about Moses coming down from the mountain with the Ten Commandments in his arms and finding the children of Israel worshiping the Golden Calf. Moses was so mad he shattered the holy tablets and shouted, "You must decide this day whom you will serve." Something like that. I noticed I was saying to myself, "You know, Jones, you've got some decisions to make yourself." That evening I drove back to Berkeley alone in my old Chevy. The events of the day and the themes of my life were much on my mind. And then there was light in the car. The car was filled with a light I could not explain except to call it God's own light. You are welcome to say it was only a headlight from an oncoming car, but I chose not to. It was not a particularly bright light, more of a glow, and it was not frightening. I remember I prayed something like, "Here I am God, help me." That was it. The whole experience lasted hardly a minute.

I don't make too much out of it, but it's there in my memory. I own the happening and what I made of it. I am glad to own it.

By itself, it would not have meant much. But given the time it happened and the issues I was struggling with, it had a profound effect. You can see why I was happy to learn, some years later, that someone as brilliant as Blaise Pascal also had an experience of light. Since then a number of people have told me of "seeing light." When I tell them I saw it once too, they often smile with relief to know they are understood.

The second memorable experience happened when I was sick. I had some brain surgery about ten years ago to correct a disorder in my pituitary gland. What they did was stick a probe through my nose, piercing the bone, to hit the front part of the pituitary. Then they shot a freezing solution through, just enough to destroy some of the pituitary, but not enough to wreck it all. At least that's what they hoped. Recovering from the operation involved a three-day headache and questions of the worst sort. Did it really work? Are there any side effects? Did it affect my eyes? That, by far, was the lowest point of my life. I couldn't eat, I couldn't sleep, I didn't feel like talking. People came and went as if in a haze. I was beginning to wonder if it would ever end. A minister friend came by for a friendly visit. A priest told me a raucous story to try to cheer me up. It didn't. Finally, at just about the worst time, my father-in-law came in. He, too, is a Presbyterian minister. We went to the same seminary, but we are from different ages. We have little in common theologically. In fact, he probably won't like some of the things I'm writing in this book. But none of that mattered that day. He approached the bed, took my hand, and began to pray. No stories, no chitchat, just prayer. His voice was steady, his grip was firm, his faith, I could tell, was real. I don't know what he prayed, but with the "amen" I relaxed. I know for a fact it was at that moment I began to recover. You can say it was a coincidence, that I would have recovered anyway, and I won't argue with you. But I still hold that experience as an instance of the healing touch of God. My own ministry to the sick has been influenced by it, for now I know how it feels to be ministered to. I realize what people are saying when they tell me, "You'll never know how much your prayer meant to me." It happened to me. I experienced it. It's as simple as that.

Experience. It is one thing we have full title to. No one can take it away from us. Beware of religionists who try. Experience cuts through theological disagreement. My father-in-law and I have something together that all the theology in the world could not provide. It is all right if two differing theologies understand the same experience differently. In this case, I'm not sure they do. Dad Harrison and I are pretty close on this one.

So God, in all wisdom and mercy, has made it possible for us to establish vital contact with the heavenly kingdom by means of the real experiences of our earthly lives. Yet notice, no particular experience is necessary in order for this to happen. Every religious community contains a pluralism of experiences of God. The creeds and documents of Presbyterianism can't begin to explain all the experiences of God that have occurred within the Presbyterian Church. I am sure this is true for all the other denominations and traditions. Faith and belief arise out of a huge pool of authentic human experience. There is no way to restrict it or even capture it forever. God still speaks to people in "divers" ways. All communities of faith are joinings and sharings of vastly different, deeply personal experiences of God.

It is OK, then, to see light or not to see light. It is OK to meditate or not to meditate. It is OK to feel God's abiding presence, and it's OK not to. The fact that we don't always experience God does not mean God is sometimes absent. If there really is a God, then we can easily afford to let each one have his or her own experience of God. We will understand our experience as we share it, as we allow others to share theirs, and as we compare all of this with the experience of those in the long tradition of faith.

· 6 ·

Supreme
But Not Absolute

People are sometimes surprised to hear me say things the way I do. They expect preachers to always sound like they're preaching. They don't expect a lot of honest struggling from us. They tend to expect answers and we tend to oblige. But most of the clergy I know are rich in questions. We wonder. We doubt. When we get together at our clerical gatherings we sometimes let our hair down and say what we know and feel, but then we go back to our churches and make it sound like God caused everything to drop right out of the Bible into our laps. I think there are a lot of people who could benefit from knowing that the leaders and interpreters of the faith are also grapplers. Most of us are working on our own questions even while we are trying to answer the questions of others. This gets difficult sometimes, and so we preachers begin to play it safe intellectually. Thus, everyone misses out on something vital.

I'll never forget the warning we received in seminary. "You can preach on racial justice, you can preach on conscientious objection to the war, but you're a damn fool if you preach on the first chapter of Genesis or the doctrine of the Virgin Birth." Well, I'm a damn fool. I preached on both in my very first pastorate. The elders called me down for it. "Those are ideas for you to discuss in seminary," they said, "not something to preach to the people."

I'm afraid this is a prevalent attitude, even while I admit those sermons of mine were not too well conceived or executed. There is pressure in the church to favor traditional concepts and phrases. The church is the conservator of the culture's past glories. I'm glad it is so. But this is also a trap. It keeps us stuck in ideas that were barely adequate a hundred years ago. I still get requests to try to do something about the teaching of Darwin's theory of evolution in the public schools. When I tell these good folks that I think evolution should be taught, they wonder how I can be a minister. When I tell them I don't think the Bible means for us to believe that this old world had its beginning four thousand years ago after God had worked on it for six days, they wonder how I can be a Christian. And when I tell them I take the opening verses of the Bible as a hymn of praise to God the Creator and not as a lesson in paleontology, they are sure I am possessed by something awful. It gets tiresome rehearsing the Scopes trial over and over again. After a time, we preachers just stop responding with our best knowledge and information. It is a sin very close to the unforgivable, but we commit it.

It is hard, almost impossible, to get people to try on a new idea. Still, it must be done, or the church will fade further and further from relevance. One idea which troubles me is the description of God as One who is all knowing, all powerful, all loving, in fact all everything, supreme and absolute in every aspect. From such descriptions I get the idea of a God who sits out there someplace, perfect and powerful, in stark contrast to all these material worlds spinning and floating around which God is supposed to have made. First of all, given present theories of a "curving" reality, where is "out there"? No matter how far you go in one direction, we are told, sooner or later you will end up coming back where you were from exactly the other way. Where, apart from all that is, can God reside? And what about all the change, movement, and uncertainty which are so evident? If God is in any sense involved with that, and the faith teaches God is, then God must tolerate change, include processes, and be affected by growth. What I am suggesting is that in God's relationship to us and the creation, the divine attributes of wisdom, power, goodness, and love, are supreme all right, but they are not *absolute*. That is to say, God is not unchanging, not unaffected by people, events, and the universe at large, all of which exist in God and are superseded by God.

I make this suggestion because I am convinced that Christian belief cannot affirm humanity, unless it also affirms the whole of nature, the entire cosmos. Nature is a rough and flexible harmony, not a strict ordering of things and events. In nature, a line is never exactly straight, and nothing, including the activity of electric particles, can be predicted with total accuracy. There is order and there is surprise in nature—predictability and creativity. New things keep happening. New arrangements form in the galaxies. New species appear in tiny test tubes on earth. The only way I know to understand it is to say God includes all of this, and God supersedes it all.

I see the relationship between God and the creation as being roughly like the relationship we have with our blood cells. We contain them, limit them, and can, under certain conditions, exert some control over them, but they also have characteristics which indicate they lead "lives" of their own. We include them, are influenced mightily by what they do, but we also supersede them. All beings, all creatures, all elements of creation, are "cells in the body of God," as one theologian puts it. These "cells," as all cells do, have a certain freedom. In the higher forms of life, choices are made which are real choices. They can affect the outcome of important happenings for better or for worse. God rejoices and suffers in this. It is impossible for the Creator not to be affected by what happens in the creation. The bond between them is too close, the total reality too dynamic.

The idea that God is influenced, changed even, by events in this and other worlds may be difficult for some people to consider. It doesn't sound quite orthodox. And yet, is this not a central biblical theme? The Bible presents a God who moves, broods, seeks, bargains, reconsiders, and sometimes regrets and even repents of a deed. God chases after those who seem hell-bent on deserting their best and highest impulses. When one thing doesn't work, God tries another. God adjusts. God makes new covenants which are continually broken but which God continually renews. In several places, God is said to change the divine mind. John Calvin, that great anchor (some would say millstone) of Protestant theology, speaks time and again of God's "accommodation" (Calvin's word) to humankind. If God were not willing to bend toward us, the argument goes, we would be utterly lost. In the Bible, God works, God plans, God chooses, God directs, God complains, God chastises, God counts hairs and grains of sand, God notices fallen sparrows, God maintains the swirling galaxies, God brings all things to completion. It is a helter-skelter situation, and God is involved. God is affected by what happens. Surely the biblical evidence for saying this is as great as the evidence for saying God is unchangeable, all of orthodoxy notwithstanding.

One of the highest expressions of what I've tried to say may be in the great cathedrals of the Eastern Orthodox churches. There the arches and the domes seem to be all of a piece. Everything bends and curves and flows. There are no sharp angles. Worshipers are enclosed in a room which wraps them together under the figure of Christ who, so conceived, is the one in whom and through whom all things were made. The architecture does in space and line what a famous Bible verse does in words, "All things hold together in Him." Such rooms are metaphors of the kind of universe I have been trying to describe. It is a universe in which the human place within the processes of nature can be accepted and taken seriously. It is a universe in which God is majestic, supreme, but not aloof. It is a universe that can be tested by scientific or other nonbiblical methods without developing serious cracks for those who stand within the tradition of biblical faith. It is a universe in transition, moving freely, even creatively, to some extent on its own, and yet it shows forth patterns and structures which lead our minds toward understanding and our hearts toward God. It is a universe in which it is not utterly fantastic to believe God has paid us a visit, for it is a universe which is part of the "body" of God. It is a universe in which we are ultimately much safer than it might seem, for God is involved in every trend, event, and happening. In such a universe, it makes a lot of sense to say, "God so loved the world. . . ."

· 7 ·

No Exception

The phrase we left dangling at the end of the last chapter goes on to say, "God so loved the world that he gave his only Son. . . ." Christianity is focused on a belief in a divine visit. Jesus Christ is God and Savior. This is a classic Christian statement. If we try to avoid it, we are avoiding Christianity itself. Christian faith is faith in Christ.

That being said, we must quickly add that Christians, over the years, have devised many ways of saying what it means to have faith in Christ. The early centuries of Christian theology were given pretty much to trying to figure out just how to say Jesus Christ is God. There were those who said Jesus was divine in spirit or soul, but human in the flesh. Others said he was born human but became divine during one of the events of his life, at his baptism, for example, or at the crucifixion or resurrection. The church has steadfastly resisted every attempt to divide Christ up into divine and human parts. Christ has been considered to be fully God and fully human from beginning to end.

I believe orthodoxy has been right to insist upon the wholeness of Christ. Jesus was not God masquerading as a human being. No. The tradition has always been that Christ is God in human flesh. "The Word became flesh and dwelt among us. . . ." What we are talking about here is the Doctrine of the Incarnation. It is central to the faith of the church. It tries to explain how Christ is the embodiment of God on earth. It is the doctrine which arises out of the Christmas story. That's a good thing to notice right there. Doctrines can arise when there are questions about what the stories mean.

When we look at Bible stories today, we are struck by the vast difference between the world view we find there and our own. In Bible times, the universe was thought of as a sort of three-decker affair. Up above were the heavens, in the middle was the earth, and down underneath was the place of darkness and gnashing of teeth. Between heaven and earth there was a certain traffic. Angels came and went with their messages. God's own voice was sometimes heard, and at other times signs and wonders appeared which guided those on earth. It was an up/down arrangement. The three different realms were different in nature and substance. Though apparently frequent, the communications between the realms were special, awesome happenings. Beings from one order of reality entered into the other. Finally, when the time was ripe, Christ "came down" from heaven. God's own Son, the very nature and being of the Creator, was born a child on earth. It's a lovely and powerful story, and I don't wish to question its basic thrust, but it is told in terms of a world view which we can no longer retain. Thus, we must ask, what does it mean to say Christ came to earth in a day and age when the universe can no longer be thought of in terms of up and down, when heaven as a *place* above the earth is impossible to conceive, and when our world is known to be a tiny part of a huge system which we barely comprehend?

Our understanding of the Christmas story, and all the biblical stories, must take seriously what has been discovered about the universe since Bible times. If we don't do this, the church's teachings on all subjects can only become less and less influential. I admit that this leaves us with difficult decisions to make about how we say important things. I admit to a basic resistance to deciding some of these things. But sooner or later, the decisions must be made, for compelling changes in our view of the world have been upon us for centuries, and the changes continue apace in our own time.

When I look at this situation, I quiver at what it implies. We are going to have to let go of some cherished expressions. We are going to have to come up with new and strange-sounding phrases. I don't see any way around it.

Under the ancient world view it was possible to think of God entering the human scene from a realm of reality that was utterly different from the world. Christ came to earth from heaven and ascended back into heaven from earth. Thus, we had this unique glimpse of the heavenly kingdom. We had a visitor from the outside. Christ came to earth to give us an opening into heaven. He delivered us from this "world of woe," making us fit for the "ivory palaces." His divinity is known in the greatness and uniqueness of it all. So goes the traditional way of telling about Jesus. But what if reality is all of a piece, as the scientists say it is? What if there is no other realm up there, as in fact there could not be if reality is round instead of flat. What if the basic processes at work in our part of the cosmos are the same processes at work in all other parts? What if the huge, more or less consistent whole Carl Sagan talks about is our true environment? In such a universe there is no possibility for an intrusion from another realm of reality, because there is no other realm of reality. Everything that is is connected to everything else. There is no "place" in such a universe for Christ to come from. There is no way to speak of God coming to us from outside the system. We must speak, rather, and it sometimes causes me to tremble to say it, of God being made manifest from within the systems and processes by which we live and move and have our being.

Given what we now know, God cannot be thought of in terms of an entirely different order from the rest of reality. The Apostle Paul, in an admittedly uncharacteristic passage, says some things in support of this position at the beginning of his letter to the Romans. Those who fail to acknowledge God, he says, have no excuse, for all they need to do is look around them for manifestations of God's life and presence. And so, perhaps, even to Paul, God was not completely unique in terms of the substances and processes of this world. We must go on to say, I feel, that God is no exception to the principles, processes, and structures of the cosmos. As they are knowable, so in a sense is God knowable to the human heart and soul and mind. God does not capriciously break the laws of physics or set aside the constant order of the spinning worlds. Whatever we can know about the divine order will be known from within the creation as God has made it and as God sustains it. God contains it all. God transcends it all. But so far as we can tell by any rational method, God does not violate the creation. God does not suspend the normal workings of the system. God does not intrude, because God is already always present, involved, moving with the flow. The divine nature "shares our common lot" is the way one modern statement of faith puts it.

Thus, though I feel shaky to say it, I feel it must be said: the coming of Jesus Christ is not an entirely unique event. It is an event in a particular time and place which demonstrates what God is doing in all times and places. The Advent is not an aberration. Christmas is not an unthinkable intrusion, not a beauty made more beautiful by being preposterous. No. It flows naturally out of the way things are. God has never been aloof and separate from the reality we know. Christ shows just how close to us God truly is.

Christ expresses the ever-present unity between God and the creation. And, since Christ is truly human, *the* "human being" one contemporary New Testament scholar calls him, we are shown that the unity between God and the world includes the unity between God and humanity. We are not separate from God in any basic sense. The relationship between God and Christ reveals the essence of what it means to be human. "You are no longer heirs, but sons . . .," Paul said. In Christ's sonship, our sonship and daughtership before God are made manifest. Christ's incarnation reveals the incarnate nature of us all and of all existence. "We are one in him," Paul also said. Yes, one in him, one with him, and in that unity, one with all that is. "I have a star at elbow and foot," sings the Welsh poet Dylan Thomas. Such visions are possible in a universe in which the divine presence is a connection among all beings and things. Christ's incarnation reveals the incarnate nature of all reality. He shows us the direction and purpose of the huge environment of which we are a part. Christ is a supreme instance of every instance. Christ is one who manifests love on an infinite scale from the one all-worthy and gracious God.

· 8 ·

Sin in
the Pumpkin Patch

H ere someone says, "You talk about love and oneness and all
that, but there are a lot of things wrong around here. Doesn't
the Bible say something about sin and evil? What do you make of
that?"

You bet there are a lot of things wrong. And the Bible does relate
the wrongness to what it calls sin. I guess we had better deal
with it.

Sin, in the Bible, is basically missing the mark, getting off the
right track, falling away from the ways and purposes of God. The
Bible declares we are all involved in this. We live in a sinful
situation, but that does not take away the responsibility we have
for our own sinning. The Bible assumes it is possible for us to know
God, please God, and live according to God's desires for us. We
can sense a good, deep, grounding relationship with the Almighty.
Anything that threatens this relationship is sin. Sin causes us to feel
cut off from God and puts us into conflict with each other. Thus,
sin is both a personal matter and a pervasive social reality. It is a
willful disobedience toward God that manifests a deep struggle in
the soul and ends up breaking the sacred agreements which bind
the community together. Sin reveals an inner hatred toward God
and neighbor, the outcome of which is often extremely painful.

Suffering may not be so much a punishment for sin as its natural result.

Preachers from biblical times on have been fond of making lists of sins. Moses came down from the mountain with a list of ten big ones. They range from spiritual attitudes and practices to everyday dealings with people. Love of God, love of neighbor, is the ancient summary of the law which Jesus reiterated. It has been taught in one form or another by many of the world's great religious leaders. Paul had several lists of sins with gossip and insult often on top. This is understandable, for Paul spent a lot of time trying to keep peace in churches. The medieval fathers listed seven deadly sins: pride, avarice, envy, gluttony, anger, lust, sloth. Poet John Ciardi, translator of Dante's *Divine Comedy,* points out how at the least we cannot be guilty of all seven at once. Pride doesn't mix very well with sloth, nor with envy, when you think about it. If you're really proud, you don't have much to envy. Avarice and gluttony tend to cancel each other out. We can take heart. We probably won't ever fall into all the sins at the same time.

Christian teaching often says that the direction of sinning is from the inside out. It is what comes from our hearts, Jesus said, that defiles us. This may be why the medievals put pride first. It has long been considered the chief motivation for sinning. We were taught in seminary that pride is the basic sin. We think too highly of ourselves. We put ourselves ahead of God. It has a good, clean, sermony sound to it. But my experience has been like that of W. B. J. Martin, the pastor of a large church in Texas, when he says, "I'd say offhand that what ails most people today is not pride but lack of it." When something like that comes out of Texas, you have to pause and take notice. He goes on, "I am constantly confronted with people who are selling themselves short. . . . What cripples their lives is not pride but a sense of inferiority." Yes, I too am so confronted.

In the old days, one's sinning had the feel of storming the heavens and shaking a fist at God. The list of sins we might suggest for our time is far less heroic. Superficiality might be number one.

We care more about image than reality. How about mediocrity, triviality, busyness? How about worry? And then there's preoccupation with ourselves. A great many of us seem to be on a continual self-satisfaction kick of one kind or another. About the closest thing we have to pride is smugness. We're Americans, so we're okay. Just don't rock too many boats and our troubles will go away. In every community I've lived in, this has been a prevailing attitude. I think we might be better off with the more traditional list. There, at least, a sin was a sin. "Sin boldly," Luther said, "but believe more boldly still." A really good, healthy sin called by its rightful name can be the occasion for a life-changing step in the right direction.

That, really, is the main point of the biblical approach to sin—it's bad, but something can be done about it. At a crucial point in Psalm 51, the psalmist says to God, "Against thee and thee only have I sinned." That puts the matter where it belongs. Sin is not just a moral lapse or a human weakness, it is a theological structure. Awareness of sin is awareness of God. That's why it's helpful to see our troubles this way. When we relate our troubles to our sin, we have related our troubles to God. Sooner or later, that is what must happen. We must recognize the divine interest and involvement with all parts of our lives. While that makes our wrongs all the more serious, it also puts us in a better position to get help than we would otherwise be in. When we relate our sins to God, we find we are not just a bunch of listless moderns drifting in and out of problems. We find we are not just blobs of protoplasm that got sidetracked by accidental events. We find we are responsible beings capable of choosing, capable of sinning, capable of feeling the effects of our sin, capable of hurting when we damage precious relationships. To see ourselves as sinners is to know all this. To know it is to be able to get something done about it. "Father, I have sinned against heaven and before you," the Prodigal said upon his return home. But before he could finish his speech, his father had embraced him, reclothed him, and shouted for the party to start. To see ourselves as sinners is to begin to move back to our true home. It puts us in agreement with God about who we are and what we have done. Such agreement can feel like a warm, welcoming embrace.

I'll never forget the time when I was a boy and a young friend and I got caught in a pumpkin patch stealing pumpkins. It was almost Halloween, and my friend said to me, "Bring your wagon after school. I know where we can get some pumpkins." I did it. We were out in the middle of the huge pumpkin patch loading the wagon as fast as we could when the cops arrived, sirens blaring, lights flashing, and, it seemed, weapons drawn. We were caught with almost a whole wagon load of pumpkins. We told the police that the lady who owned the field said we could have them. Trouble was, she was the one who had reported our crime. They gave us a good dressing down and told us we could each take one pumpkin home. We left in a hurry, the wagon with two average-sized pumpkins in it bouncing along the rutty road. I went right home and began to carve my pumpkin. Pretty soon my father came up the walk. "Where'd you get the pumpkin?" he wanted to know.

"A lady gave it to me," I said, which in a way was true. He didn't ask any more questions, and I didn't give any more answers.

Now my father was well known in our small town. Chances are he had played gin rummy with the chief of police that very afternoon. Chances are the chief had told him that I had been caught red-handed in the pumpkin patch. So he knew, and I knew he knew, and he knew I knew he knew. And so there was that barrier between us. I was keeping a secret which was already known, and I knew it was known. That's dumb, but I did it. It was only a year or so ago that the subject came up again. The friend who had been my accomplice and I were together for a high school reunion, and we began to talk, in my father's presence, of that day in the pumpkin patch. "Were we scared!" we said, and all of us laughed including my father. But in a way it wasn't funny. The barrier should have been dealt with much sooner. For a long time I had sacrificed a portion of my experience of love and respect from my father by keeping my "sin" to myself. It's the way sin works between people. And it is the same way with God.

· 9 ·

"He Stops It Right There"

Every Sunday, in tents, storefronts, white frames, brownstones, or modernistic glass-and-steel cathedrals, the church proclaims: "Christ has come to save us from our sins." It is at the heart of the good news. It is proclaimed in prayer and sermon and song. Not always, however, are we told what it means to be "saved from our sins" or just how Christ might accomplish it. Let's give it a try.

First of all it means we take sin and evil seriously. They are real even if they are not the whole story. It means that sin and its effects don't go away because we want them to. A young man who grew up in a prominent Christian home in colonial Virginia wrote in his journal, "I committed uncleanness with Annie the maid for which God forgave me, and then we had tea." That doesn't quite catch the sense of the biblical idea of sin and redemption. On the other hand, sin is not the end of the world either. God is. The Bible is not a book about sin and punishment; it is a book about God, whose love and mercy keep things whole. In the theological sense, at least, we are not made of eggshells. No matter how broken we become, we can be put back together again. We are redeemable. Human wrong is not the controlling characteristic of human life, serious and pervasive as it may become. The main point in the biblical doctrine of sin is that sin is forgivable.

We can easily get bogged down in a morass of hopelessness and helplessness by dwelling on our sins. I've noticed that often the prayers of confession at the beginning of worship services are so burdened with references to sin and evil that it becomes impossible to get much out of the brief assurances of pardon which follow. In fact, sometimes the choir sings the assurance. We have laid our huge mess before the Lord, and the choir gives a lovely response, and that's supposed to do it. I think a lot of worship hours are lost right there.

Furthermore, we preachers seem to have been more adept at coming down on the sins than we are at lifting up salvation. Sometimes we make so much of sin we put ideas in people's heads. A substitute preacher came to our church once and listed in his sermon fifty or sixty sins mentioned in the Bible. One of our vibrant ladies thanked him for introducing her to a few she had never heard of before. And then there was the lady who remarked to her new pastor, "Reverend, before you got here, we didn't know what sin was."

The main thing about sin is that it is forgivable. The main thing about a broken covenant with God is that it is renewable. Our position before God is as one who is party to a contract that we are likely to break, but no matter how many times we do, the contract is renewable at our option. Not that this is always easy. Pain is involved. The cross of Christ is a demonstration of the pain sin can cause. And the cross is the place where we see how far God will go to forgive us. Even out of our sinning, great unities are revealed. The cross stands for the worst things human beings can do, and yet it becomes a vehicle for God's grace. Our sense of God's oneness and love is never more disrupted and never more firmly established than at the foot of the cross. It is not inevitable that sin capture and control us. In Christ, the church proclaims, God has set us free from the bondage of sin. The greatest of evils, painful and destructive as they are, can become opportunities for renewing our oneness with the living God.

Over the years, several theories have arisen to explain just how Christ's crucifixion saves us from our sins. They are grouped, in theological talk, under the Doctrine of the Atonement. That word "atonement" is interesting in itself. Notice the unity implied, the making one again of what was broken. I'm not sure, however, that any of the theories are as helpful as they sometimes claim to be. One of them uses the Old Testament rite of animal sacrifice as its main image. The unblemished lamb is brought before the people and lifted up. The people identify with the animal through the prayers and ministrations of the priest. Then the animal is killed and offered on the altar. It represents the people's offering of themselves in contrition and humility. God accepts the offering, and the covenant is reestablished. The people are again right with God according to the ways laid down for this to happen. From early times, the church has said that Christ on the cross is the Lamb of God who takes away the sins of the world. He has become the sacrifice which renews our bond with the righteous One. In faith, we identify with Christ and are saved. These are powerful images, primitive as they are. I am not sure, however, if many of us today can enter fully into a theology which is based on the sacrifice of animals.

Another theory says that Christ was our substitute. We belong on the cross, not Christ, but God substituted the Son for us. This "satisfied the debt" we owed for our sins. Still another theory begins with the phrase "He died a ransom for many." Christ paid the ransom so that we could be free from our captivity to sin and death. There are other theories of the atonement as well, but they all, it seems to me, try to say more than can really be said. To whom, for instance, is the ransom paid? Some say to God. But that leaves God paying God. Others suggest the Devil, but then we have God in some kind of deal with the Devil to transfer accounts. And, in the first place, what kind of God needs blood sacrifices to satisfy a sense of justice? Too often, the theories about how Christ saves us have made a shambles of our ideas of God. We need to look for other images.

One of the best I've ever heard came in a sermon preached by a church executive in New York City one snowy day when our seminary class had gone to visit the denominational offices to learn about the church's mission program. As I recall, we got stuck on the George Washington Bridge on the way home and didn't get back to Princeton until two in the morning. But it was worth it. I have never forgotten the picture the preacher gave us of how Christ accomplishes his saving work. He spoke of a battle in the Arab-Israeli war and told us that in the midst of the battlefield there happened to be a Christian chapel. Among its appointments were some marvelous wood carvings of the twelve apostles and an especially striking carving of Christ. The carving of Christ, in fact, had been done on the stump of a tree that was still rooted and protruded through the floor of the chapel. As the battle raged, the chapel was hit by shells and was almost destroyed. All that was left was the tree-trunk carving of Christ standing in the midst of the smouldering mess. Hunks of the carving had been blasted away. Big chunks of shrapnel were imbedded in the figure of Christ. Rocks, sand, and bullets had peppered the carving, burrowing deep into the wood. "That," said the preacher, "is what Jesus does. He takes into himself all the hate, all the violence, all the sin we can dish out, and he stops it right there. He takes the evil of this world into his own body and lets it go no further." I still carry that picture as one which helps me understand what Christ does on the cross. When Jesus cried out, "Father, forgive them, for they know not what they do," he lifted the wrong from those who drove the nails into his hands, from those who had conspired to have him crucified, and from all of us who, in our own way, help them. Our sin, bad as it is, is not too much for Christ. He takes it into himself, stops it right there, and makes it into a possibility for life and hope.

We can experience this through confession. Confession ties our particular brand of sinning to God's forgiveness in Christ. A powerful vehicle for this can be the Confessional of the Roman Catholic Church, where the sinner sits with a priest who hears and speaks the words of grace. That the Confessional is not always well used is beside the point. One priest is supposed to have said, "Hearing confessions is like being stoned to death by popcorn." My feeling is that the Confessional or something like it is a good way to formalize the confession process. Protestants are left with general prayers of confession and counseling programs. We would do well to focus this much more sharply.

We have far too many people in our churches who hear and believe the good news of the forgiveness of sins but who do not feel forgiven. Too many feel God is ashamed of them, that they haven't measured up, that they are living in sin. Divorce, the breakup of families, griefs and losses of various kinds, failures, fallings, rejections: these experiences seem especially able to trigger a sense of guilt. Yet these are life events, experiences which come our way, struggles we have to live with. Many people who are doing the best they can still feel guilty. Added to the normal pain is the pain of self-condemnation. Christ wants to stop that. Christ is able to take all that into himself and stop it right there. The way we come to know and believe in Christ's forgiveness is by confessing to God, by doing what we can to make things right again, and by talking with other people about this experience. It seldom happens all at once or once and for all, but the painful guilts of our lives can be handled, and Christ can help. He died for our sins. By focusing on that death, it is possible to see our sins begin to die. Being forgiven is letting Christ stop the guilt process running rampant within us. Later we will talk about a specific prayer which seems to work right at this point.

· 10 ·

Human Anger | Holy Wrath

W e have been speaking about God's unbounded love, about the unlimited possibility of grace and forgiveness, about the huge reservoir of kindness in God's heart which gives rise to the gospel. But the biblical prophets tell us that God gets angry. That may be why we don't like them. They say things like, "Because you worship at the altar of silver and gold, the Lord is getting up the divine dander. Because you see injustice and do nothing, the Lord waxes hot beneath the collar. Because you look down your stylish noses at the poor, the Lord is looking over his list of punishments." Who wants to hear stuff like that? You don't. I don't. The children of Israel didn't those many years ago. Yet those things were said, and they were meant to be taken seriously.

Listen to old Jeremiah:

> *But the Lord is the true God;*
> *He is the living God and everlasting King.*
> *At his wrath the earth quakes,*
> *And the nations cannot endure his indignation.*

And again:

> *Behold the storm of the Lord!*
> *Wrath has gone forth,*

A whirling tempest;
It will burst upon the head of the wicked.
The anger of the Lord will not turn back
Until he has executed and accomplished
The intents of his mind.
In the end of days you will understand it clearly.

Jeremiah writes like one with a penchant for starting the day from the wrong side of the bed. He's a heavy, the kids would say, almost always on a downer. Anyone with a God like that has to have something wrong with him, wouldn't you say? Some of the learned scholars have suggested that Jeremiah was just depressed. But that won't work, for there are also Isaiah, Hosea, Amos, Joel, and a host of other major and minor prophets who proclaim the wrath of the Lord. In the Bible, the God of love gets angry.

But the God of the Bible does not get angry for no good reason.

Because your guilt is great,
Because your sins are flagrant,
I have done these things to you.

Thus, Jeremiah quotes God to the people. God gets angry because we sin, fall short, allow evil to go further than it otherwise would. But this isn't as fearsome as it might sound. There is a huge comfort hidden in this idea. God's anger has a purpose. It is not a whimsical thing. It does not come and go, as so much human anger does, without warning or reason. It has a definite cause and direction. Furthermore, God's anger is *limited*. It is limited, at the very least, by our evil, which though great and painful, is not infinite. The holy wrath is directed toward finite evil and is limited by it. God's temper is never out of control.

God's anger, Jeremiah says, accomplishes the intentions of God's mind. This anger, then, is a rational force. It is not to be confused with the mindless eruptions of human passion we read about every day. Nor is God's anger to be equated with the great natural or humanly contrived catastrophes we suffer. Granted, the Bible speaks of four common images of what God's wrath is like—floods, fires, earthquakes, and storms. It sounds like the subjects of a recent rash of movies. But more than once, the biblical writers take care to tell us that God is not in these things. These are pictures of what can happen when we try to toss off our limits. It can be a disaster. God's anger reminds us that we can't go on a destructive way forever. The holy wrath is almost a natural consequence of human evil. "This is the condemnation: Light was in the world, but men loved darkness rather than light, because their deeds were evil." To displease God is a terrible thing, worse than being caught downtown when the earthquake hits. The worst thing that can happen is to be on the outs with God. As the prophets see things, the disaster stories are barely strong enough to carry the weight of terror that can come upon the unrepentant soul.

Some contrasts become clear. Our anger can lead to mindless destruction. God's anger is the desire to set evils right. Our anger arises from a sense of having been wronged or slighted. God's anger is directed toward the restoration of justice. Our anger is often the desire to get even. God's anger acts on behalf of peace for all. These distinctions could save us from buckets of trouble. Anger that is directed toward what is truly evil, which is limited by that evil, which is for the purpose of generating the energy to oppose the evil, and which is mitigated when its purpose is fulfilled, that kind of anger is holy wrath even when found in the human breast. It can be among the most creative forces around.

There is another welcome distinction between holy wrath and most human anger. Notice what it says in Psalm 103:

> *The Lord is merciful and gracious,*
> *Slow to anger and abounding in steadfast love.*
> *He will not always chide,*
> *Nor will he keep his anger forever.*

God's anger builds up slowly. God doesn't explode all at once and scare us hopelessly out of our wits so that we can't straighten up and fly right even if we want to. That's what I do to my daughter whom I dearly love. I explode all of a sudden. I wish I could take my cue from God. God counts to ten a hundred times. God warns us as the divine patience grows thin. If only we could control the pace of our anger, if not its magnitude, we would stand a better chance of changing what we're mad about for the better. God does not blow up. God lets sparks fly, the psalmist says. God lets us know a fire is being kindled. There is time for helpful impulses to act. Destruction is not the inevitable outcome of God's wrath.

And God is quick to get over being angry. Isaiah quotes God as saying

> *For I will not contend forever,*
> *Nor will I always be*
> *angry. . . .*

Merciful and gracious is the permanent condition of God's heart, the Bible says. God's anger is a temporary episode in the midst of that condition.

> *His anger is but for a moment,*
> *But his favor is for a lifetime.*

How much happier it would be if we could do with a grudge what God does with the divine wrath—get it out and get it over with and go on.

"The secret of anger is care." I lift this phrase from Rabbi Abraham Heschel's marvelous book on the biblical prophets. Because of care, God's anger is ultimately redemptive. It is a form of blessing. Even in anger, God does not deny the divine nature which is mercy and steadfast love. Anger is part of living. It is not wrong to get angry. To live in this world and never be angry is impossible. Those who feel, those who love, those who grieve, those who have compassion, those who work for justice, will also get angry. It would do us good to model our anger after that of the Bible's God. We might pray a prayer like this: "Help me, Lord, to pace my wrath as you pace yours. Help me to give a warning to those upon whom my anger is likely to fall. And above all, help me to leave my anger behind and remember my grudges no more, even as you have forgotten the troubles I have caused you." God's anger, according to the Bible, is that which saves us when all else fails. A scalpel. A healing. A twinge of pain. Would that our anger was the same.

· 11 ·

"Charged With Grandeur"

I am sometimes puzzled, sometimes saddened, sometimes amused, by what people seem to think they have to believe in order to be a Christian. There are utterly preposterous theories about the beginning or end of the world, for instance, that get presented as if they are basic church doctrine. And then there are the miracle stories of the Bible. I am seldom more discouraged than when I see a bright, questioning person cut himself or herself off from the faith because they think if they don't accept the miracle stories in a certain way, they are not fit to believe in God. I have had people ask me right out, "In order to be a Christian do I have to believe that Jesus walked on the water? Just actually got out of the boat and walked on the water? If I have to believe that," they'll say, "I'm in trouble. I just can't swallow it."

The answer to the question is no, you don't have to believe Jesus walked on the water in order to be a Christian. In order to be a Christian you have to believe that Jesus Christ is lord and savior, and there are several theories about what that entails. But let's talk about the miracles for a bit, and especially about the New Testament miracle stories.

In the universe we know about today there is little room for "intrusions" from another sphere of reality. God is not "someone" separate from the processes in which we live. This way of seeing things takes us out of the usual situation in which the miracles are

understood. That situation tends to assume two spheres of existence, ours and God's. A miracle is said to occur when God inter-
venes in our sphere. For a moment, at least, God is said to break
the rules of nature for the sake of this or that cause or person or
group. I wouldn't insist God *can't* do this. It is just that God *doesn't*
do it. God doesn't set aside the processes of nature so far as we can
tell by any recognized method of investigation. Therefore, whatever
we mean by miracle, we don't mean that anything goes so long as
God is doing it. No, we assume that even God plays by the divine
rules of the universe.

The trouble with some of the traditional understandings of miracle is that they wreck any notion of a consistent ordering of nature.
They make God into a rather handy being who jumps to this or
that human request or, worse, acts on the basis of some divine
whim. And yet, the Bible is full of miracle stories. The gospels show
Jesus performing them. And I hear good, intelligent people of faith
tell about the "miracles" which occur in their lives today. Experiencing miracles is a significant part of Christian faith, and I do not
wish to diminish it. But neither do I want to live in a universe
where someone else's prayers or the changing desires of God can
stack the cards against me. I always feel strange when I see athletes
make religious signs at a crucial time in a game. Is God really going
to favor them over those who may be praying on the opposing
team? I feel strange about it, but I can understand the feeling, for
I welcome any help I can get, divine or otherwise, when it comes
to a three-foot downhill putt that breaks to the right.

When we look at the New Testament miracles we are looking
at stories which were obviously precious to the early church. They
have been precious to the church over the centuries. But there is
something about those stories we must become aware of if we are
really going to understand them. In New Testament times, the fact
that a person performed a miracle did not necessarily mean that
person was divine. In those days, the power to perform miracles was
thought to be available to many people, some of them quite ordinary folks. We have, in fact, references in the gospels to miracles

performed by the Pharisees who turned out to be the enemies of Jesus. Jesus himself said that some of those who cast out demons and did other mighty works in his name would be told to depart from him. He would treat them, he said, as if he never knew them. So it becomes very clear that in the first century the ability to work miracles was not considered unique. One thoughtful writer has said, "That a man possesses strange power which I cannot understand is no reason why I should receive his teaching as divine oracles of truth." That is a good safeguard for us in these days when many miraculous claims are being made just as they were in olden times. Not all of these claims are as scrupulous as we might wish, and some, even though made in all sincerity perhaps, have led to destructive results.

To understand the New Testament miracles, then, we must look beyond the mere fact that they were recorded. Jesus did not, the gospels show, perform miracles in order to amaze people. He often told those he helped or healed to keep it a secret. If the miracles are not recorded to show that Jesus was divine, what is their purpose? The faith of the early church is that the miracle stories reveal the deep, inner, unfolding purposes of God. For New Testament Christians, the significance of the miracles lies in their connection to the Kingdom of Heaven as Christ proclaimed it, not in their value as unusual wonders, or as "proofs" of Christ's divinity. There was nothing unusual about them in their original context. Miracle stories abounded. For the people of those times it was not important to say a miracle happened. What was important was to show the purpose, context, and meaning of the miracle.

The miracles of Jesus take place in the context of the biblical expectation of the dawning of the messianic age. The prophets of old had spoken of one who would come to make the lame walk, the blind see, the prisoners free. Even more than this, it was assumed that God's chosen servant would have power on earth to forgive sins, interpret the scriptures, overcome evil, and gather a community of servant people. In the miracles of Jesus, we see these expectations being met. When Jesus heals a lame man, he asks, "Is it easier to say your sins are forgiven or rise, take up your bed and walk?'' He links his power over the paralysis to his power to forgive sins. It is as if the one reveals and confirms the other. When Jesus casts out demons, the evil spirits bow and tremble before him. Long before the disciples recognize Jesus as the Christ, the demons have acknowledged his power over them. The stories become part of the larger picture of Christ's mission in the world.

In the opening of blind eyes and the unstopping of deaf ears, Jesus is shown as the light of the world for those who have eyes to see and as the proclaimer of God's truth to those who have ears to hear. When Jesus calms the storm, he saves the little church, and I like to think, given the size of the congregations I serve, all little churches. When he comes walking on the water, he shows he will not leave us alone on the stormy seas of life. And when he feeds the multitude, he shows he will be known in characteristic fashion in the breaking of bread. The common biblical metaphors in which light can stand for God, bread for God's blessing and provision, the sea for the realm of uncertainty and danger, and sickness for sin, are woven into the miracle stories. Christ is shown as revealer and guide and helper in all the situations of life. The meaning of the stories derives from their setting in the biblical witness to God's gracious activity. Accounts of miraculous happenings take place in the context of a larger "miracle," the "miracle" of God as God, the "miracle" that God is love, the "miracle" that God's love is being made known. The stories show Christ to be one who focuses the activities of God in the world. The specific miracles as recorded point to the great miracle of God's unbounded love, which is the source of life's meaning and happiness. *It is this larger "miracle" which Christians must take seriously whether or not they take the miracle stories literally.*

In the Bible, this larger "miracle" is expressed in the two great miracle stories, the exodus from Egypt and the resurrection of Jesus Christ. God's whole enterprise almost ended at the edge of the Red Sea, but God found a way through. Again, everything was over as Christ was laid in the cave and the stone was rolled in place. But somehow Easter happened. God moved through the obliterating situation. The church gathered. Christ was experienced as present in all fullness and power. The promise to Abraham had not been defeated. Through him and his descendents, all the world can still be blessed. These normative, controlling stories reveal God as the One who is not defeated. The processes which make for life do not come to a sputtering end. Out of the worst disasters, new possibilities are born. It may not be apparent as the hard things happen, but over the long pull the evidence piles up in favor of God who, as the hymn says, "is working his purpose out." The priest-poet Gerard Manley Hopkins begins a poem with the line "The world is charged with the grandeur of God." That this is so, and that we can sense it, imagine it, be awed by it, be blessed by it, and participate in it, even while life clobbers us, is miracle enough for me. In the totality of the grandeur, I am happy to have the miracle stories of the Bible, for they link me to countless others who sense in all things the awesome reality of God's grace at work.

· 12 ·

See How Sneaky I Am

Sometimes when I begin to interpret the miracle stories the way I do, or the creation stories, or some of the other more fantastic parts of the Bible, people accuse me of taking the Bible as just another book. They feel I am somehow downgrading scripture if I use the same kind of interpretive methods upon it as might be used in the interpretation of Shakespeare. They will say, "The Bible is the Word of God and not to be tampered with. Change any part of it and you destroy it all." My reply is that modern biblical scholarship does not seek to change the Bible, but to know more of what it means. Every statement of biblical truth is also an interpretation of biblical truth. Interpretation is a human process. The Bible is made up of human words and has come to us through a process of human interpretation. The church believes in its very heart, however, that somehow God's Word comes to us in those human words and interpretations. This issue may be the one which troubles the church the most right now. It is the question of authority.

The great divisions and many of the small ones within Christianity occur over this question. It is why we have Catholics and Protestants. The Roman Catholic position is that Christ's authority passed on to the Apostle Peter and then to the succession of Popes. Protestants say that when Christ said to Peter, "On this rock I build my church," he meant Peter's faith was the rock, not his person. So

Protestants claim Christ's authority abides in the people, in the believing heart, and in the fellowship which gathers in faith. It is a crucial matter, for authority in the church means authority to say what the scriptures mean. It is authority to say what God's Word is in any given situation. I am sure the majority of Protestants have little understanding of this issue. It mystifies them. "After all," they say, "I can read, and there it is in the Bible in black and white." Well, maybe so, but we sure get a lot of crazy stuff out of the Bible that way.

Most Protestants in this country seem to believe that the Bible must be taken in its strictest, literalistic sense. This principle of interpretation is relatively recent. It arose in all of its glory during the westward expansion of the American frontier when traveling preachers expounded for hours, often in fearsome ways, on the basis of texts in English translations of the Bible. That Hebrew and Greek words lie behind these texts did not concern them. My father still says to me, "Bob, the trouble with your preaching is that you don't scare people enough." But one of the reasons he hardly ever goes to church is that as a boy he was subjected to the scariest kind of preaching they could come up with in Bicknell, Indiana. Base those scary images of fire, smoke, and stench on a literalistic interpretation of holy writ, and you've got a powerful way to drive people into heaven, or, as in the case of my father, out of the church. Thank God other ways of interpretation are available.

I am to the point where I resent it when those who disagree with my interpretive principles try to imply that I therefore don't take the Bible seriously. My reply is that I take the Bible too seriously to take it all literally. Things are not true just because they are in the Bible, but many things are in the Bible because they are true. So much of it was never meant to be taken literally in the first place. In the Bible there are poems, little novels such as *Jonah,* parables, embellishments of historical events, several versions of the same happenings, and there are just plain old obscurities which the centuries have covered like sand covers tracks. Therefore, I'm always suspicious of attempts to cite a list of scriptural texts as a way of

proving points in sticky contemporary issues. Such lists are prevalent right now in the debate over women's rights and the squabble
about homosexuals. Before we get the Bible's message on questions
like these, a lot more has to happen than the mere citing of a verse
or two.

At the very least, we must ask, What did this text mean in its
original setting? To whom was it written? By whom? For what
purpose? When? Many times, the answers to these questions will
determine the text's meaning. We must ask what were the historical and cultural forces at work at the time? Did the text come from
the leader of a party or a faction or a divergent point of view? If
so, can we identify the writer's enemies? Against whom, or in favor
of whom, was the passage written? What community of faith might
the writer belong to? The answers to many of these questions are
not easily available. Bible scholars work on them and argue about
them. We should be aware that such discussions take place. This
doesn't mean that we ordinary people should not read, mark, and
inwardly digest passages of scripture. We should do that. But we
must not think that what we find in the Bible on our own is the
truth of a certain passage for the whole church. We need to be
humble about what the Lord shows us from out of the Word, as
well as grateful. Sadly, Bible verses have become little theological
spitballs that Christians throw back and forth at each other across
the aisles of their disagreements.

We preachers are at fault in a lot of this. We have not equipped
people with an adequate theology of the Word. For the most part,
in an effort to proclaim what the Bible says, we avoid the issue of
what the Bible is. It leads to a lot of fluff. We are fluff peddlers,
and the people in the pews are left without a sense of where
authority lies. We duck this issue because people so often misun-
derstand. People want things clear and simple. It is much simpler
to say, "God created the world in six days," than to say, "The *Book
of Genesis* does not tell us much about the beginning of the world
and the origin of life, but it does tell us a lot about the Creator of
the world and the Sustainer of life." Unless we give people credit

for being able to deal with the Bible this way, I feel we do them a grave disservice.

Jesus said, "All authority in heaven and earth is given to me." Our authority is Christ. To me, this means that Christians interpret scripture from the point of view of faith in Christ. The life, death, and resurrection of Jesus become keys to the meaning of other passages. Thus, we take some passages of scripture as being more important than others. I don't see any way around this. All Bible verses do not have the same weight for faith and practice. If they did, we would be lost in endless quandary.

In the Old Testament, for instance, there are a number of food laws. Certain things, when eaten, render one ritualistically unclean, unfit for worship, and in need of special prayers. Succulent pork chops and delectable crab legs were on the list. Most of us, I hope, are willing to say, "The New Testament repealed these laws. Pass the platter." Another regulation made good, healthy sex between a husband and wife an uncleansing act. We have no trouble, I assume, seeing that in Christ, such regulations, even though they are not specifically mentioned, are repealed. But let's go on. The Old Testament seems to condone slavery, and the New Testament doesn't say much more about it. "Slaves, obey your masters," said the Apostle Paul. Jesus said as much himself. Does this mean we are not to oppose human slavery? Are we to justify this kind of bondage on the basis of scripture? No. No. No. No. No. Why? Because it became clear in the church over the years, and especially in the mid-nineteenth century, that nothing as dehumanizing as the American slave trade can be reconciled with God's disclosure of truth and love in Jesus Christ. Jesus told slaves to obey their masters, but in the name of Jesus, the church eventually told masters to free their slaves.

How do we explain such a situation in terms of the Bible and its authority? We explain it by saying that God's Holy Spirit led the church to a fuller truth than the scriptural record allows. That, I agree, is a huge step to take, but we have to take it. We must, with fear and trembling, acknowledge our departure from the letter of a particular text in order to fulfill the spirit of the entire gospel. We must do this in all humility, recognizing that the truth we find may not be the final truth. We must pray and struggle and meditate upon the texts of scripture, and then we must exercise our judgments and take responsibility for them. We must develop sound interpretative principles in order to draw God's Word out of the ancient writings, so that God's Word can live in our hearts and influence our lives today.

When I read the Bible in church, I introduce the reading with a phrase like, "Now hear the Word of God as it is found in Holy Scripture." No one catches it, probably, but what I have done is to make a distinction between God's Word and the book on the lectern. I have said, as Jesus implied in his parable of the soils—and as John Calvin came out and said plainly—the Word of God is known by proclamation and hearing. God's Word is not something that sits on a shelf or a pulpit or in one's coat pocket. The Bible contains God's Word as it was written down in olden days. But God's Word has life and power today in ways the writers of scripture could never foresee. "Hear the Word of God as it is found in Holy Scripture and," I might add, but don't, "in other places as well." See how sneaky I am.

We preachers need to get over being sneaky about this. People need to grapple with the way biblical authority works. The Bible did not drop out of heaven full-blown. There were centuries of oral tradition, then the collecting of scrolls, then editing and cutting and arranging in order. The Word of God as found in Holy Scripture cannot possibly be considered as fixed, rigid, obvious, or unyielding by anyone who knows the tortuous route by which the scriptures came to be. Still, this collection of books and pamphlets we call the Bible is received by the church as holy, set apart, special in authority and influence for faith and practice. Even though we now know that much of what the Bible says about God, faith, life, sin, or salvation is culturally conditioned, we still believe that these writings reflect the core of the truth we must come back to time and again. From its setting in ancient culture, the central message of the Bible somehow gets through to us today. The record of the faith of the fathers forms and informs our faith. In the Christian church the search for the truth always begins with a diligent search of the scriptures. But it must not end there. What Jesus said to the disciples he also says to us: "I still have many things to tell you, but you are not ready for them now. The Helper, the Comforter, the Spirit of truth about God will come and lead you to the truth."

· 13 ·

Authorities

If authority in the church isn't confined to the Bible, then where does authority come from? How are people supposed to know what is true and what isn't? Not everyone can study Hebrew and Greek and other ancient languages in order to know what the scholars are doing. How do ordinary people get at what is true in the faith? Is it sort of to each his or her own?

The Roman Catholic Church has evolved a solution by vesting teaching authority with the world-wide community of bishops over which the Pope presides with full authority. The Pope has the final say, and in the churches that is a great authority.

Protestants go about it differently. As so often happens, one break with the central authority has led to other breaks. The Reformation, for all its power and necessity, has left a fragmented expression of Christian faith in the Protestant churches. This makes the problem of authority much more difficult, but it doesn't have to end up with "to each his or her own."

One of the churches I serve is connected with the congregationalist tradition, which stems from the Puritans of New England beginning back in the seventeenth century. This is an independent group, I tell you, with ruggedly individualistic ways of church life. No creed can be imposed on anyone from outside the local setting. Each congregation draws up its own statement of faith and covenant of church order. An old saying around congregationalist churches is that the existence of God depends on a majority vote of the members at a duly constituted meeting. Well, it's not quite as bad as that. There is a sense of community and history. The basic teachings of faith in a triune God, Father, Son, and Spirit, are central. The Bible is very important. But no one has the right to tell anyone else what he or she must believe. The inviolability of the individual conscience before God is staunchly defended. This leads to a democratic way of church life. There are authorities rather than a single, all-embracing authority. It calls for an internal balancing act to keep everything in place, but I think something like this is necessary no matter what kind of spiritual authority one accepts.

Churches are usually organized around one of three principles—rule by bishops, rule by elders or other leaders elected to act on behalf of the members, and rule by the congregation as a whole. In the first group are Roman Catholic, Orthodox, Anglican, Lutheran, and Methodist churches, though there are varying degrees of reliance on councils in each one of these. The second group includes the Presbyterian bodies and most all of those churches that have the word "Reformed" in their names, their model being Calvin's Geneva. The third group is sometimes referred to as the "free churches." Congregationalists, Baptists, the Disciples of Christ, and a host of independent and pentecostal groups are organized this way. All three systems of mediating church power can be justified by New Testament texts. To my mind, features of all three should be included in any great merger of churches, and the time for that to happen may not be too far off.

At any rate, what we are saying is that along with the Bible, the church is also an authority for our faith and practice. When Catholics say the church preceded the scriptures and produced them, they are right. The very task of choosing the books which we consider sacred was not completed until the fourth century A.D. But Protestants are right to emphasize that scripture shapes, forms, and corrects the church. Scripture comes out of the church and speaks to the church. The history of the church is, in a sense, an extension of the New Testament story, but, as it must, the church has always held to the biblical record as a special, constitutive witness to God's ways. It is much the way we Americans, at our best, hold to our Constitution as the formative document for our way of life. There is scripture, and there is tradition, and the two cannot be completely separated. Scripture guides the tradition, but it guides from within the tradition as it moves and changes. We *interpret* scripture, we never just read it. There is no getting back to the pure, unspoiled structures of New Testament Christianity. The fact of the matter is that such structures did not exist even in New Testament times. Much of what we have as teaching on the way things should be ordered in the church came in response to squabbles the apostles found themselves enbroiled in. Furthermore, Protestants have to remember that the bulk of the Christian tradition is a Roman Catholic one. Our slant on the truth is relatively recent, so we need to affirm the continuity of interpretation going back to biblical times, even as fresh insights come to us in our time.

Thus, we have scripture, tradition, and one thing more, our own experience. We live with a three-sided authority. We must have the humility to listen to the teachings of others who speak to us from within our tradition. We must study, contemplate, and ponder the scriptures, trying to hear what the Bible says. But we must also have the courage to own our very lives before God. We must never deny our ability to catch glimpses of fresh truth. And we should not be deterred from making our unique contributions to the ongoing movement of the church's faith. All three authorities operate upon us. We need to play fair with them all. Our experiences, visions, and callings need always to be checked out in scripture and tradition, but what is taught in the Bible and the church must not make meaningless what we know from the responsible living of our lives. Each of the authorities is corrected by the others. They are sources of truth in spiritual things. The Bible and the creeds of the church guide us along our pilgrim way. They do not dominate our souls and minds with teaching which could only be valid in some other world. They mediate our experience of God in this world.

I find people often need this kind of approach in order to keep their faith during crises in their lives. Take, for instance, divorced persons who desire to remarry. If they accept an all-authoritative literal Bible, they must consider themselves adulterers if they act on their desire. Believe it or not, even in this day and age, I talk to people who are deeply troubled about this. They are in love, they have a chance for a new life with someone they care for, a new family is being born out of past suffering, but the Bible calls it adultery. Is that the Word of God for them at this point in their lives? I admit it sounds like tampering with holy writ, but I don't think it is in the deepest sense, when I say, "Look into your heart. Do you feel that what you want to do is forbidden by holy commandments?"

"No," is almost always the answer. "I believe God wants us to have a second chance. But there is that adultery business written right there in the Bible. What can we do?" And so with fear and trembling I sometimes feel compelled to move with a person beyond what the Bible says at this point to what, in the wider experience of the church and in the painful experience of the person's life, becomes for that person a new authority. The new authority takes as much of the old authority into account as it can. The new authority is not a license to do as we damn well please. But the new authority, arrived at over time and trepidation, often guides us away from older, harsher teachings which, if enforced literally, would increase the suffering of a suffering soul. Surely, when we look at the sweep of the scriptural witness, the best of the church tradition, and the truth-laden crises of our lives, we must believe in God's mercy, compassion, and forgiveness, or we would all be lost. We come to see through it all how the loving God of the universe does not desire people to suffer further loneliness, regret, and guilt. And we notice how, in story after story, in scripture, tradition, and life, the characteristic activity of God is to bring something good out of something bad. Surely, no teaching is meant to stand in the way of that possibility. And so, if divorced persons find they can love again, surely they can become free to feel, decide, and act upon that love. Their freedom comes from the context and blessing of a knowing, loving God.

"The letter kills, the Spirit makes free," says Paul. If you think this makes it too easy, try it.

· 14 ·

"The Holy Spirit Hopped the Fence"

From time to time we have mentioned the Spirit or the Spirit of God. In the church's faith, these are not just casual expressions; they are linked to basic understandings of God's nature. These days there is a lot of talk about the Spirit. The radio preachers urge us to be filled with the Spirit, led by the Spirit, touched by the Spirit. It can sound kind of spooky if you're not acquainted with the background of such phrases. They derive from the vital part of church doctrine found in the third section of almost every creed, the section on the Holy Spirit.

In the New Testament, the Holy Spirit is basically the Spirit of Christ sent in a fresh way to continue what Jesus started. The Holy Spirit is also closely tied to the church. However we organize it, however human it may seem, the church is a divine creation gathered and energized by the Spirit. The Holy Spirit in the Church, informing, correcting, enabling, inspiring, is Christ's continuing presence on earth. When Martin Luther said, "We are Christs to each other," he expressed this sense of the close bond between the ministry of Jesus and the activity of the Spirit. The Spirit encourages us to be for each other what Christ is for us all. Thus, the main Christian creeds, naturally enough, put their statements about the Holy Spirit and their statements about the church in the same

section. "I believe in the Holy Spirit, the Holy Catholic Church. . . ."
The Spirit of Christ is the foundation of the community of faith.

So the Holy Spirit is not something spooky. We do not have
some free-floating ghost which comes and goes by the pressure of
mysterious whims. There can be nothing true of the Holy Spirit that
is not true of God revealed in Jesus Christ. We are to "test the
spirits," according to New Testament warnings, against the claims
of those who say they act or teach "in the Spirit." The test is the
life, ministry, death, and resurrection of Jesus Christ. We are also
to notice the "fruit" borne by those who serve in Christ's name.
The good fruit lasts, preserved, so to speak, by the Spirit.

When we talk about the Spirit, it is impossible to miss the
dynamic, related qualities of God. In fact, one of the early ways of
thinking about the Holy Spirit was in terms of the relationship
between God as Creator and God as Redeemer, the relationship
between the Father and the Son. The Father loves the Son and the
Son loves the Father and the Holy Spirit is that relationship of love
between them. This inner, divine love, the old formulation says,
sort of splashes over onto the world and the church. I kind of like
that. It shows God being much more than a smooth, self-contained
deity. There are swirly places here, scars and tangles where the
vastness of the universe and the wild varieties of human experience
can get caught. Through the Spirit, God is involved in everything
that's going on.

Several theologians over the past generation or two have related
their thoughts on the Holy Spirit to the idea of evolution. From
Darwin's work with biological evolution there emerged notions of
"creative" or "threshold" evolution. This recognizes that from
matter, somehow, there came life, and from life came consciousness,
and in consciousness there has arisen an awareness of love. The
suggestion is made that God's Spirit is active at these thresholds,
prodding and pulling the universe and its creatures toward the
discovery of all embracing, unbounded love. The movements and
changes of the universe, it has been said, are in this direction, and
the giver of life is involved in it all. At the very least, these notions

remind us that the Holy Spirit is a deeper and wider reality, even, than the energy within the church or the bond between the persons of the Trinity. Holy Spirit is God alive and moving from beginning to end. Holy Spirit is a cosmic force, a reality of divine relatedness which applies not just to Christian persons and holy things, but to all persons and all things. "And the Spirit of God was moving over the face of the waters," the Bible says just before God speaks the words "Let there be light." That hovering, brooding Spirit relates the divine, creative Word to everything from the very beginning. Nothing exists outside that Word. "Nobody and nothing can escape the presence and the power of God the Holy Spirit," says one theologian; "this is a given of the Christian experience of life 'in Christ.'"

It is fitting that the biblical words for "spirit" are also the words for "wind" and "breath." Life, movement, energy, growth, inspiration, imagination, inner meaning, changes of heart, the huge upheavals of life and history, the sparrow flying or falling and the feelings with which we behold either, the turning of the earth upon its axis, the sense of smallness in gazing at the stars, this, that, and everything else we can name, are related, connected, and made significant by that "breath" which breathed life into Adam, by that "wind" of which we hear the sound but do not know from whence it comes. Holy Spirit. The cosmic Spirit proceeding through the cosmic Christ. We find we're not alone in our earthly home. Never were, nor shall we ever be. Nor must we depend on mysterious interventions from another realm to make us feel safe. In the Spirit from whom we can't escape we are part of what God has been involved with since the beginning. "The force that drives the water through the rocks/Drives my red blood," sings Dylan Thomas. The poets have always known that trees can clap their hands, that floods can speak, that there are sermons in the very stones. It is a unified universe. Our imaginations do not completely betray us when they leap to connections behind the jarring inconsistencies of life. The Greek philosophers, the Hebrew prophets, and from what I can tell, the best modern scientists share a basic assumption about the Truth. It is that the Truth is One. If we are taught by the Spirit, we learn more and more about this essential oneness, and we are drawn closer and closer to its core.

Therefore, while Christians find the Holy Spirit active in the church, and while we experience the Spirit's full influence there, we must try not to limit the Holy Spirit to our eccesiastical structures. The history of Christianity can be read as the church's attempt to build a fence around the Holy Spirit and, in the words of a fine preacher I know, in noticing how the Holy Spirit "hops the fence." It happened right at the start when Paul, after a time of settling down from his conversion, went to Antioch to work in the church there along with Barnabas. All of a sudden the little church began to grow. Greeks and Jews started to worship together. It became clear that the Christian way was not going to be limited to one group. The church discovered a new life apart from its place as a sect within Judaism. This caused the Mother Church in Jerusalem to shudder. The leaders of that congregation did not know what to think about such an unexpected development. Furthermore, Paul and Barnabas were proposing that they go off in all directions to proclaim their faith and share their experience. There was no preventing them. The Holy Spirit had hopped the fence.

Fence-hopping is still characteristic of the Spirit. In every instance where people are breaking down racial, national, ethnic, social, or religious barriers, the Holy Spirit is on the move. The new concern for justice for women is an activity of the Spirit. The Holy Spirit will not allow us to be complacent about what we know and believe concerning the worth of all persons. The Holy Spirit does not permit us to be comfortable with our prejudices. The Holy Spirit is forever jogging us loose from our religious and cultural ruts. Someday, the Holy Spirit will lead us to express our Christian faith in a unified way. "We are one in the Spirit, we are one in the Lord," says one of our newer hymns. That oneness needs to find a home on this side of heaven. Someday, God's Holy Spirit, whom Christians experience as the Spirit of Christ, will lead all people into one great fellowship around the whole, wide earth. That may be too much to expect right now, but it is not too much to pray for. So far, the Holy Spirit has hopped a lot of fences. I believe the Holy Spirit will hop a lot more. And I pray for this to happen.

· 15 ·

Variations on a Theme

W e have spoken of God, Jesus, Spirit. This leads to the idea of the Trinity, an idea deeply embedded in the Christian tradition. It is not the easiest thing to try to explain, and in fact it may be beyond explanation. Christians have been accused of believing in three Gods, but they always insist they believe in one. GOD IS ONE is as basic to Christianity as it is to Judaism or Islam. The unity of God is never denied in the biblical religions.

Christians don't have three Gods, but Christians have experienced God in three distinct ways. There is God the Creator and Sustainer, the One in whom all things exist, the One whose nature is love and whose chief known characteristic is relatedness. This One is present in the ups and downs of living, participates in the trends and developments of history, is involved in the ways and actions of nature. This One shines forth in all that is, supersedes it all, pushes it all to its next moment, receives it all back, and is influenced by it all in the process. There is none greater than this One to be conceived and none firmer to be believed. Our worship and devotion, when directed to this One, are accepted, perfected, preserved. The one, true living God is worthy of our deepest thoughts, strongest feelings, most purposeful actions. We do not live apart from this God whether we know it, acknowledge it, or not. Nothing else to be said about God changes this sense of who God is.

Then there is the self-disclosure of this divine reality focused in the Son. The Son reveals what human nature truly is and truly can be. In the Son we see our potential and our calling, and we are reminded of our falling short of God's desires for us. The Son confirms that God's purposes are not defeated by human evil, bad luck, or personal tragedy. From crosses new lives and new communities can come. The Son fulfills all prophetic utterances which proclaim that justice and peace are not just human causes—they are divine longings. It is in the Son that all outward things have their beginning and end. It is in the Son that all things hold together. It is in the Son that we experience the closeness of the Creator. The Son is consistent with the Creator, entering the creation on the Creator's behalf and on ours. The Son lives his life on earth on the same terms as everybody else. Thus do we know him and understand him. Thus is it made clear that we are known and understood. The Son personifies at a certain time and place the presence of the great God who everywhere and at all times speaks and accomplishes and orders and suffers and moves and prevails through divine and infinite love.

Finally there is the human, earthly response and connection to God's outgoing love. This is the experience of God as Spirit. The church holds that "in the Spirit" we worship, believe, pray, and serve. We have tried to suggest that the Spirit connects us, eventually, to all people everywhere, to all who ever lived and died. The Spirit gives us awareness of that connection so that it is not just a doctrine, but an experience. So does the Spirit give us assurance that we are forgiven, received, welcomed into the fellowship of the people of God. And the Spirit gives us hope for the ultimate victory of God and for our participation in it.

From the earliest of times, the God of the Bible has been known in these three ways. It is unfortunate that the doctrine of the Trinity got caught up in a sort of numbers game. I can't help but think that we have here one of those instances when theologians have tried to overexplain the faith. The Trinity has been used to explain the place in Genesis where God, getting ready to create us humans, says, "Let *us* make man in *our* image." Why does God refer to divinity in the plural here? It is a question Bible students have wriggled with for years. "Well," some of the answer-bearers say, "this refers to a heavenly council attended by the three persons of the Trinity." That's really much too neat. It is also terribly high-handed to take a fourth-century A.D. formulation to explain an Old Testament text dealing with the beginning of the human family. A better explanation is that the plurals here reflect old notions of heavenly beings with whom God can converse. The Trinity is not something by which to explain troublesome texts. It is rather a sort of summary doctrine that expresses the ways people have perceived and experienced the one, true God.

It is not necessary to believe in a certain theory of the Trinity in order to be a Christian. It is not even necessary to believe in this or that theory of the two natures of Christ. During the early centuries of the Christian church, these matters were argued about and fought over, often bitterly. As a result of such controversies, two great councils were called together, one at Nicaea in 325 A.D., and another in Chalcedon in 451 A.D. The statements which came from these meetings have been bellwethers of orthodoxy ever since. But this is not as confining as it may seem. Everything has its story.

Christ is fully human and fully divine they said at Nicaea, of "one substance with the Father" is how they put it. Often these statements, or others much like them, are used as tests for authentic faith. If you don't accept these things this way, you don't qualify for communion in such and such a church. Sad. For history has given us other formulations to lay beside those older ones. Further-more, a case can be made, as Alan Richardson does in his little book *Creeds in the Making,* for saying that the council fathers struggled for a sense of inclusiveness. The desire may well have been to rule out as few people as possible. The final formulations tended to affirm both sides of the main argument. What the struggle showed was that those who could believe Christ divine but had trouble with his humanity, and those who saw Jesus as human but flinched at some statements about his divinity, had a larger task than formulat-ing a creed. They had to find a way of accepting as brothers and sisters those who wanted the emphasis on the other side. So do we.

If the creeds leave the door open to various ideas about how the two natures of Christ fit together, so they allow for a number of ways to talk about how the three persons of the Trinity are related. Here the battle was mainly between those who saw the Trinity as a sort of hierarchy of Father, Son, and Spirit, and those who pushed for an equality of status. The discussion still goes on. For us today, the Trinity can be a way of talking about God's diverseness, relatedness, and openness. God stretches, perhaps, and is even torn a bit on behalf of the creation and its creatures. God is not a self-contained reality off in the distance. God is involved with us here as Father, Son, and Spirit. All praise.

Like the Bible, the creeds are among the standards we must take seriously. They are beauties and treasures of the tradition. But they are not axes and chopping blocks by which to get rid of honest seekers and questioning believers. Furthermore, the creeds, like the Bible, have historical settings. They are influenced by the thought-forms of their times. I do not believe the Spirit binds us to the formulations of a particular century, even the first century, for guidance in belief. I believe the Spirit frees us to receive in our time and in our terms the same force, enthusiasm, and devotion which the faith brought to people of former times. If life is of a piece, and nature and the universe too, then so is history. The exact formulations of the great creeds may not ring as true to us as they did for those who first heard them, but they point us to a faith which was alive and moving in days gone by just as it is today. I don't like to think of nature or history admitting of great aberrations, but there may be, like in a good jazz performance, some surprises along the way, which, before all is done, are experienced as satisfying variations on the original theme.

· 16 ·

"I Think I Can
Fit in There Someplace"

It's almost funny sometimes what comes over the telephone. Within a few minutes I can have one call from someone requesting that I say in five words or less what our church stands for and another call from a person complaining that what we believe sounds too cut and dried. In the old days there were orthodoxy trials where people were forced to give a certain account of their faith or be excommunicated or something worse. In some sense, it can happen still. There are always those who feel the circle of faith should be drawn rather tightly, and there are others who like to see openings in the boundary. Over the years, councils have met and given their answers to the questions of belief. Orthodoxy derives from the accumulation of statements which these councils produced. Many of these statements are beautiful expressions of Christian teaching. Others are marvelous examples of the human capacity for splitting hairs. I accept the statements of orthodoxy as guides, but I do not feel bound by their language. It could be argued, I suppose, that this makes me a heretic. But I don't think it does. My experience is that belief comes in fits and starts. It waxes and wanes. At certain times of life some beliefs are more important than others. As I get older, for instance, I'm less interested in God the Creator and more interested in God the Sustainer. I need help to keep going. The thought of starting over from the beginning seems a little far-fetched to me, and a little scary. Often the noble desire to have a measure of control over what constitutes authentic belief results in the oppression of the human mind and spirit. Theology can get in the way of a person's development. And yet, I'm not willing to say, "It doesn't matter what you believe just as long as you're sincere." I've listened to a lot of sincerely held tripe.

One place where councils meet to test for something like orthodoxy is in the process of ordination to the professional ministry. Almost every Christian body enforces some standards at this point. In the churches I belong to, the main responsibility for this is in the hands of other ministers. One might add, for better or for worse. There usually comes a time after seminary, after some form of internship, and after a church or church-related agency has issued a "call" for the person's services, that he or she must submit a statement of faith and purpose to the church's authorized body. Then the candidate for ordination must answer any and all questions that might be forthcoming. This, to say the least, is a harrowing experience.

I'll never forget the time it happened to me. It was in northeastern Pennsylvania in early October, a most beautiful time of year. I was picked up early on Tuesday morning to journey far into the countryside for the meeting of Presbytery. A Presbytery is composed of the ministers and representative elders of the churches in a given area. It has power like that of a bishop. We drove through the blazing woods, past dairy farms and orchards, crossed brooks, skirted lakes, came close to Camptown, the famous racetrack where the ladies are supposed to sing "Doo da, doo da," and finally came to a village where the largest structure was a fine old white-frame Presbyterian church with a marvelous spire and huge green doors. In there I met my trials for ordination. The morning was spent with the committee. They wanted me to read and translate some Greek and Hebrew, to tell about the "offices" of Christ according to the Westminster Confession (Prophet, Priest, and King, I believe they are), and they had me name the four boards of the Presbyterian Church which existed at that time. I forgot the Board of Pensions, but I hope the Board of Pensions doesn't forget me.

After a hefty Pennsylvania lunch of chicken and dumplings, I was presented to the entire Presbytery, about eighty "Fathers and Brothers" gathered in the church sanctuary. (I don't think there was a sister in the house. This was back in 1959.) The questions were straight and to my liking until, toward the end, a wise-looking teaching elder, that is to say in Presbyterian talk, a minister, rose and asked, "Do you believe in the resurrection of the body or the immortality of the soul?" Just by the way he asked it, I knew this was the one they would make up their minds on. I decided to stay close to the scriptures and quoted the Apostle Paul in several places. The seed falls to the ground and dies, he says, so that the new plant can grow. But he also says for us not to worry about those who are "asleep." I went through a song-and-dance about how the two notions are really the same, and that seemed to satisfy them. Then they asked me if I had any questions for them, and like a fool I said I was concerned over what it meant in the question I would have to answer during the Ordination Service: "Do you believe the Constitution of the United Presbyterian Church in the United States of America to be the form of doctrine contained in Holy Scripture?" My question was about the word "the" in the phrase "*the* form of doctrine." Does it mean "the only" form of doctrine contained in holy scripture, or does it mean "one of the" forms of doctrine so contained? Well, you never heard such a blustery discussion. The fathers and brothers went at it hot and heavy for at least half an hour. "Why no one has ever called attention to that before," one of them said. He seemed indignant. Another was afraid that if we took the more exclusive position, we would be leaving the Methodists out, and he had to work with the Methodists, because they and the Presbyterians were using the same church building in the little town he lived in. The arguments mounted on both sides and in all the positions in between. Finally, I raised my hand and said, "Mr. Moderator, if it be the desire of the Presbytery, I am sure my views can fit in here someplace." With that the trials were arrested, as they say, and a motion carried to authorize my ordination.

I have always appreciated that experience. It showed me how doctrines aren't really very much unless you take people into account. It showed me how the church that was about to ordain me was more diverse and flexible than it might seem. I think this may very well be true of a lot of churches. It showed me that earnest believers, leaders of the churches, trained in different times and places than my own, could disagree about some basic teachings and still include each other in the warm embrace of Christian fellowship. Therefore it was particularly satisfying when, on the Sunday evening after that meeting of Presbytery, many of those ministers on both sides of the argument laid their hands on my head and, with solemn prayers and joyous singing, made me one of them.

So it can be with orthodoxy. The ancient standards can be applied in ways which embrace current experience, and often are. My feeling is that even in those Christian bodies that seem so rigid and imposing to an outsider looking in, there is much discussion going on. From the beginning, Christians have exhibited diversity among themselves over matters of basic doctrine. Sometimes this has caused shameful fights. It has always caused debate and reformulation of the statements of faith. Though there is pretty much universal acceptance of God as Father, Son, and Spirit, of Christ as lord and savior, of the church as the earthly form of the divine community, these beliefs are held in a wide variety of ways. It can seem confusing at times, as if no one can really tell you just what you have to be or do in order to be a Christian. But it is because of this diversity that many of us can say, "I guess I can fit in there someplace." We can and we do.

I am convinced that the invitation to Christianity is much broader than it sometimes appears. If you are interested in the Christian faith, I think it is possible, if you look hard enough, to find your place.

· 17 ·

Nothing We Do Causes It

O nce we mention the resurrection of the body or the immortality of the soul we get into what many people think religion is all about. They think religion tells us what happens to us when we die. Religion is about much more than that, and Christianity, with its deep roots in the Hebrew scriptures, is certainly as much concerned with life in this world as in the next. When the New Testament talks about the Kingdom of Heaven, it is not talking about a place where people go after they die. It is talking about the rulership of God in this world we live in. The Kingdom of Heaven is our present task and future hope. The Kingdom of Heaven envisions life and reality under the lordship of the living, loving God.

This said, we must also acknowledge that Christianity has some things to say about what happens to us after we die. It would have to, for death is one of the universals of living, and people are concerned about it in deep and awesome says. "What do I have to believe in order to get into heaven?" This is a question I'm often asked. I respect that question. It shows the person is making a connection between this present life and the eternals beyond. Jesus was asked pretty much the same question by a very rich man, and the rich man was told to give his riches to the poor. I take this to be an indication of the significance of our earthly lives and orientations. It points to a realm of the spirit that goes beyond wealth or status and appearance. It points to a divinely placed value on the lives of each one of us, rich or poor or whatever. From this divinely placed value comes the meaning of our life and of our death.

Now a lot has been written about death and dying lately, much of it very good. There seems to be testimony favoring the view that death is not the worst thing that can happen to us. In fact, many of those who have been pronounced dead and then come back to life, speak of beauties and blessings and a great sense of peace. Whether these people were really doornail dead is perhaps a question we should raise, but I don't doubt their testimony about what happened. I have heard too many of these stories to set them aside, and they fit in with what happened to me one time.

I was only ten or eleven, maybe, and was prone to get allergic reactions to grass and dust and things like that. More than anything, in those days, I liked to play football. The rougher the better. One afternoon during a particularly vigorous game, I got my nose bounced too deep into the grass, and I came up with a snootful. Before long my eyes were watering, my throat was swelling, and my nose was a big red running mess. When I got home I didn't feel very well, so I did what I thought was the best help for everything in those days: I lay down on my bed and began reading comic books. Pretty soon I felt unable to breathe. I stretched out as far as I stretched, closed my eyes, drew in what breath I could, and let it go. I got a little scared. Something was choking off my air, but for some reason I didn't panic. I just lay there very still and soon I got drowsy. I must have been terribly quiet, especially for me in those days, for I remember my mother coming in and then going out quickly and calling my father. "Look at him," she said, "he's never been like this before." They both seemed very far away. My father, as I recall, didn't seem too worried. He was probably glad for a few minutes' peace.

During an hour or so of that quiet resting, I felt extremely ethereal, I grew tall, I sensed myself moving and hovering. I wondered if I were dying, if this was what death was like. Then there was a gentle light above me (that same light?), very beautiful, almost like a promise, a smile. I don't know how long this lasted, but when I got up I felt great. My throat was clear, my breathing strong, and I went out and played football again in the last light of the day. There is evidence around which might indicate that such experiences are premonitions, little glimpses of death. I don't know.

We do know that to make sense out of life, we have to deal with death. We have to face our own dying. Wisdom from all ages and traditions has said this is so. I find people are not so much afraid of death, but they are afraid of certain kinds of dying. Rightly so. And it is for sure we experience our death ahead of time in the deaths of others, especially those close to us. Grief is our burden of death in life. Sooner or later, we shall carry it. We will feel the sorrow of loss, and we will feel the fear that comes to us when we watch another suffer. We know we probably face pain, and if not, then something worse—a long empty time without clear feeling or perception. No one I talk to wants that. They prefer a quick dying, even if painful. As it stands now, we really haven't much to say about it, but the question has been raised in medical and theological forums. Do we have the right, even duty, to exercise some control over our end time? My feeling is that we do, but the details are far from clear.

Along with the specific and personal business of going through our last days, there is also what we make of them. I have watched good Christian folks die like dogs, and I have seen others who seemed to have little affinity for things of faith slip away peacefully and with great calm. A lot has to do with the particular illness, I suppose. But I have also noticed that there is often a quickening, a focusing at the end of life that doesn't seem to come at other times. It's sort of like meeting a deadline; or better, it's as if we can sense the Spirit's true ways most clearly at the end. I haven't noticed that Christians are the only ones for whom this seems to happen.

We had a young man in our congregation who, in the midst of some important moves in his life toward a deeper and more realistic faith, discovered he had an incurable cancer. During the year of his dying, Jerry became the spiritual leader of the church. It often happens that the one who is hurting is the one who leads us into deeper truth. We had a prayer and study fellowship that met on Tuesday nights, and Jerry became a part of it. As he became weaker, we began to meet at his home so he wouldn't have to miss. Through the various therapies, we were with him, through the disfiguration of his body, through the indignities of his ordeal. Jerry, during this time, read and prayed and grew in faith. At a meeting very near the end, his body a grotesque mixture of skinniness and swelling, Jerry spoke to us about what this time had meant to him. He reviewed his life briefly, he mentioned the events of the year just past, and he looked around the room at each of us and said, "And now you are my friends, and it has all been worth it." He died within a week. Somehow, it was like hearing the last words from the Cross. It was like being present with Jesus in the Garden when he prayed, "Not my will, but thine be done." It was like an echo of the voice of Christ telling his disciples he would not leave them alone. "It has all been worth it." I shall never forget that night.

And so was it a death that Jerry died? Was it a death when so many of us, now these many years later, still carry his words with us? Is it a death when, surely with God's help, someone makes more out of his dying than many of us make out of our living? Is it a death when so many feel more alive for having known the one who died? Is it a death when faith becomes more real in the process of dying? Was it a death Jerry died? Do suffering and crosses always leave us with dead bodies? Is laying down one's life for one's friends just a fancy name for what happens anyway? As I ponder these things, I have not only the death of my friend Jerry to think about, I have also the death of Jesus Christ. And so I wonder, is it Jerry's death, or is it, in some deep way, Christ that died? Everything about Christian faith sooner or later hinges on that question. "It is Christ that died," Paul says in Romans. Somehow it is always Christ that dies. It is always Christ who suffers. All suffering is Christ's suffering. Each death struggle is Christ on the Cross. Every death, Christ's death. Every grave, Christ's tomb. Jerry's death, our dying, and

Christ's death on the Cross are somehow connected. "It is Christ that died."

But Paul doesn't stop there. "It is Christ that died, yea rather that is risen again." He seems to say that if our death is Christ's death, our graves are Christ's grave, and Christ's resurrection is our resurrection, our hope and our life. He seems to say that this is so for us now. We need not wait until we die to know this and feel it. By facing our crosses in the light of Christ's Cross we deal with our dying, and we can discover divine possibilities for a new kind of life. This discovery can exert a profound influence upon us in our struggles on this side of the grave.

Is it a death, or is it another instance of God coming alive in a human life, even as that life ends? Easter is the church's response to that question. Easter says, "Yes, it is Christ's death you die; it is Christ's resurrection you share." Nothing is wasted. No pain without purpose. No life without meaning. No breath, no heartbeat, no sunset, no flower, no insect, no comet. Every instance charged with significance. We don't have to believe this to make it so. Nothing we do causes it. We don't believe our way into heaven. It is the way things are.

We know that one form taken by Christ's resurrection was the spiritual rebirth of his followers. The deadness inside them was overcome. They shared his death, and so they shared his resurrection. The church, in a most basic sense, is the resurrection body of Jesus Christ. There was an ending and a new beginning in Christ's life, but there was much continuity between the two. Christ, in his resurrected body, is shown going about just as he did before the crucifixion—teaching, helping, and gathering his people. The church lives and moves as the body of Christ risen and victorious in a world full of defeat and death. We are members of Christ's body, Paul says, and that is a living body come back from the grave.

· 18 ·

Principal, Interest, Carrying Charges

Another question I am often asked concerns the practice of prayer. It goes like this: If God knows all and loves all, then why pray or believe? What difference can it make? It's a good question, one that leads to the heart of the *experience* of faith. By praying we learn what it feels like to be a believer.

I have said there is nothing you or I can believe that will cause God to love us more than God already does. There is nothing we can do that changes Christ's resurrection back into a crucifixion. There is nothing we can be right or wrong about that alters the ultimate significance of all that is. God does not depend on our faith for divine existence. Sometimes I think we become too faith conscious. It is a form of human self-importance. "If only I had more faith," I hear people say, "this wouldn't be happening to me." It makes me sad to hear it, for it is often the most faithful among us who say such things. What, pray tell, can we do to make God love us more? Unbounded love is already poured out upon us. Do we really think that more faith, more prayer, more anything, can increase what is infinite? I hope not, because to think that way puts us in a frantic position. We must always be asking, "What more could I have done? What prayers ought I to have said? What alms might I have given?" These are the questions which give rise to spiritual guilt. They assume that we are responsible for things we can do little or nothing about. We must get away from the notion that we have responsibility for every matter of life or death. It is not we who hold the universe together, however faithful we are. God accomplishes that whether any of us believes or prays.

However, too often we don't experience God's deep, unbounded, freely given love. We go about our lives as if we were on our own in a big empty place. That can be scary. It can make us want to do something or believe something to make us feel safer. It may even drive us to our knees. However we get there, it is good for us to be on our knees in prayer, not so we can rearrange the universe to our liking, but so we can begin to feel our closeness to the One in whom the universe is benevolently arranged. Prayer is the experience by which our faith becomes real to us. Sooner or later, all we believe about God, life, or the universe, gets focused in a prayer. Sooner or later, everybody prays. I suppose some people have never prayed, but I have never met one of them.

A helpful approach to prayer comes from a fellow named Dave Jacobsen who has conducted Prayer Renewal Workshops in churches all around the country. Dave defines prayer as "telling the truth to God." He points out that this is the small "t" truth, the real things of our earthly lives. The prayer of Jesus in the Garden, he says, shows Jesus telling the truth to God. "If it be possible, let this cup pass from me." Jesus did not want to face what he had to face, and he told God so. That was the truth. But, in the very next phrase, Jesus is shown to have moved to a new spiritual position before God. He prays, "Yet not what I want, but what you want." So, Dave says, prayer is movement. When we tell the truth to God, we get under way. We begin a communication which can help us occupy different ground.

Dave sometimes uses a phrase that could be a signature for all I have been trying to say. "God, in great wisdom, has made it possible for the small "t" truth of my life to be the vehicle of communication with God." Using the Lord's Prayer as a model, Dave encourages us to enter into prayers which involve asking

("Give us this day our daily bread"), grudges ("Forgive us our debts as we forgive our debtors"), temptation ("Lead us not into temptation"), and agreement ("Thy kingdom come, thy will be done on earth as it is in heaven"). He urges us to stay close to our real experience. He tells us to ask for what we really want, new golf clubs, a raise, a better figure, if that's what it is. No use trying to fudge at this point, for God knows what we really want even before we ask. That's what the Good Book says.

I have found the prayer about grudges to be a most profound one. It is clear that Jesus understands us at this point. It is also clear he considers this an important prayer, for it is the only part of the Lord's prayer he comments on after he has given it. "If you forgive others," Jesus said, "then your heavenly Father will forgive you, but if you do not forgive others, then your heavenly Father will not forgive you." What can this mean? Do we create a forgiving attitude in God by forgiving others? No. God forgives. Grace abounds. We live by mercy before we start to pray. What is going on here, then, is not that we are learning how to cause God to forgive us, but rather that we are being taught how to experience God's forgiveness. The greatest block to that experience is recognized as the holding of a grudge. If we wish to feel the forgiveness of God in our hearts, we must become forgivers. God has already forgiven us all. We can participate in that forgiveness by letting go of the grudges we hold against each other.

How do we do that? Dave has an exercise which he introduces with some standard "centering" techniques—breathing, relaxing, yoga stuff which we Christians have too long disparaged. However, Dave is the first to say the exercises are not necessary. It is not important how we pray or what we say in prayer so long as it is the truth—and gets at what is important in our lives. In order to get at the truth in the prayer about forgiveness, Dave gives us four questions to ponder. The first is, What happened? That is, what did the person do to wrong me? He was walking down the street, say, and as I approached, he crossed to the other side. The second question is, What did I add to what happened? Why that dirty stuck up so-and-so snubbed me. What kind of friend is that? Third, What has to happen for me to be even? Isn't that a dandy? Don't overlook it. Chances are we have our thoughts about what getting even might entail. The first question, Dave says, represents the principal, the second the interest, and the third, the carrying charges. Then we are ready for the fourth question, Am I willing to forgive this person? Yes or no. It is not necessary to be willing to forgive. It is only necessary to tell God the true answer to the question. That is the prayer about forgiveness. It is the truth about our willingness to forgive.

I can tell you this prayer works. By that I mean I have seen people go through this process and come to the point of letting go of a debilitating grudge. I used this material once in a sermon at a church where I was the substitute preacher. After the service, I had no sooner gotten to the place where I was staying when a lady was on the phone saying she had not spoken to her sister in nine years until just a few minutes before she called me. After going through the prayer about forgiveness, she had decided to visit her sister. "Can you believe it," she said, "I no sooner started up the walk when my sister opened the door and ran down to meet me. We hugged and cried, and it's finally all over. Thank God." Yes, thank God.

The lifting of a grudge can be the most exhilarating of spiritual experiences. When it happens, we feel close to another, and we feel close to God. We are moving where God moves. God the forgiver has become a reality in our lives. This is how faith and prayer can operate. They put us in touch with the ways of God. They connect our lives to God's life. They give us a chance to experience the way things really are. It's not that we are trying to change God or the universe. No, faith and prayer help us experience God and the universe as connected and whole. They help us sense our place in it all. They make our lives, in limited and imperfect ways, feel akin to God's life.

Christianity was never meant to be an intellectual exercise. There are no secret rites to master, no tricky riddles to unwind, no body of outside truth that one must comprehend and recite. The beliefs and practices of the faith are there to help us experience the presence of God in mind and heart and soul. Worship and song, prayer and sacraments, study and service, these all relate to our sensing the reality of God in the reality of our lives. Forgiving and being forgiven, asking and giving, getting and being denied, hoping and despairing, the whole gamut of human feeling and experience is caught up in the experience of faith. As Dave Jacobsen says, we learn the answers to our prayers as we live our lives. We keep on telling the truth to God in good times and bad. When we do, it can seem like God's truth is abiding in us. It seems like it because it is.

· 19 ·

Far Better Just to Ask

"What happens when God says no? I pray and pray, but nothing happens. I never get what I ask for." Ministers hear that a lot. People feel frustrated in their praying. It can be a painful thing. My feeling is that God doesn't say "no" in so many words, but I know for certain that it can feel like it. Everyone who has ever prayed has likely had that experience. Prayer, in fact, includes the risk of having it seem like God says no. To pray for something is to take a chance. Prayer lifts everyday issues of life into the context of communication with God. Thus, if things work out badly, we not only have the bad situation in our hands, we have the possibility of feeling out of sorts with the Almighty. Sooner or later, our prayers will test our faith. If we stay with it, our praying will lead us to contend with God.

Dave Jacobsen says some helpful things at this point when he reminds us that a primary ingredient in prayer is the business of asking. Asking, real asking, is the turning over to another the choice of whether or not we get what we ask for. There's the rub, of course. We are not always clear on this score. Rather than ask, we argue, we pressure, we manipulate. So much asking among members of families isn't really asking at all. "Wouldn't you like to go to the movie tonight rather than spend another boring evening at home?" That's not a question, it's a hidden statement of what the person wants, and it includes a barb of criticism and some pressure which is quite likely to rankle. True asking allows the other person freedom to say, "Yes, I would like to go to the movie tonight," or "No, I don't want to go." Asking grants freedom. It's one of the nicest things we can do for anyone. It gives the other person power in regard to something important in our lives. Thus, when we ask God for something, we are granting God freedom at that point. We are acknowledging God's power in the matter. We are opening ourselves to possibilities other than the ones we have perceived or desired. Notice, it is all right to perceive things the way we do, and it is all right to desire what we desire, but in asking God, if it's really asking, we are letting go of some of our perceptions and desires. We are laying ourselves open for something different from what we have been able to imagine or project. We are putting ourselves in a new position before God, one which may lead to struggle before it leads to a sense of communication.

The experience of the Apostle Paul may help us here. He says in Second Corinthians that he prayed three times for the "thorn in his flesh" to be removed. There are several theories about what this "thorn" might have been. Some say it was a physical handicap, that Paul was stooped or epileptic or suffered from terrible arthritis. Others say he had a speech impediment. And still others have suggested, more or less humorously, I hope, that Paul is talking about his wife. Whatever it was, he wanted it gone, but it didn't go away. Three prayers didn't make it go away.

It may be good for us to be reminded of the limits of our praying. Our prayers do not cause miracles to happen. We do not pressure God into suspending the laws of nature. We do not cause God to feel and act toward us in ways other than God already feels and acts. Rather, our prayers put us in touch with God "who loves us, cares for us, and has our best interests at heart." That is another Dave Jacobsen phrase. Three times the apostle prayed that his thorn be removed. Three times the answer was, "My grace is sufficient for you." The third time, apparently, Paul believed God. It is to Paul's credit that it only took three times.

What can happen in prayer is that the communication itself

becomes more important than what we pray about. We pray for healing, that a life be spared. It is a good thing to do. I have no doubt that prayer can be part of the healing process. I have seen it, and I have experienced it. But sooner or later, we will very likely get to the point—and it's all right if it's much, much later—where the communication with God about healing becomes more precious, even, than the healing. And it is true, of course, that every person we pray for ultimately dies. The "answer" to the prayer for healing includes that possibility, and so it includes the possibility of ongoing communication, as the prayer for healing becomes a prayer for comfort in grief. Prayers do not heal. God heals. Prayers for healing open communication with the Healer. That communication, as it deepens and grows, becomes the healing, the salvation, the "answer," even if, as will happen, the one prayed for dies.

In Paul's prayer we could say the answer was no. The thorn stayed. But the communication was, "My grace is sufficient for you." It is, therefore, not only miracles and healing which are evidence of God's power. Paul bears witness to a thorn in his flesh that will not go away. Prayer doesn't help. Yet, in the midst of that experience, Paul finds God's grace to be sufficient. Out of pain and frustration comes a testimony to the goodness of God.

It must be, then, that any of us can qualify as witnesses to the power of God in our lives, not just those who seem strong or those whose prayers seem to be answered every time. And I can see in Paul's thorn an approach to some parts of my life which trouble me. My desk, for instance. I have a messy desk. I am embarrassed about it. I feel people won't think I work very hard when they see it. I put a card on it which says, "A clean desk is the sign of a sick mind." I promise myself to clean it up by Advent, then by Lent, by Easter, by Pentecost. It stays messy. It's how I work. It's the way I am. I have even prayed about it. If I have any communication from God, it is that I should stop worrying. I'm getting my work done. I know where things are even if nobody else does. And furthermore, in the whole congregation, perhaps in the whole world, I am the only one who really cares how my desk looks, so why give time and energy to it? By the grace of God, I can be of some use to the church and its people, messy desk and all. Our "thorns in the flesh" are not signs God doesn't love us, care for us, or hear our prayers. When God seems to say, "No, this thorn stays," it is possible there is a much larger context of grace for us to experience in the matter.

It is also possible, in our praying, that we can be left on the "outs" with God. We can have an experience that makes us feel cut off from the Source and Giver of life. I remember when I was a boy I wanted a horse in the worst way. It was an impossible wish. We lived in town, there was no place to keep a horse, and to board one out was just too expensive. I knew all this. But I still wanted a horse. When I had my tonsils out, I had a terrible time. I felt miserable night after night. I really thought I might be dying, for it seemed nothing could be any worse than the ache in my throat and ears. One night, as my father was comforting me, I said, "You know what I want more than anything in the world?" He said, "What? I'll get it for you." I suppose he thought I was going to say ice cream or something like that. "I want a horse to ride," I said. And I really did. And I said it tearfully. And my father, unable to say what he knew should be said, nodded and indicated that I could have a horse. I hugged him and went to sleep. When I got well, he never mentioned it, and I never brought it up again. I knew I had tricked him. I had tried to take unfair advantage of the situation.

Tricks block communication. Truth and sincerity communicate. This is true between us and God. If we use tricks, we get no communication, no matter what "answer" we get to our prayer. Tricks take away possibilities. They seal us away from a chance to feel close to God about something important to us. Far better just to ask, really ask, and take our chances. Asking sets the asked one free. Asking grants the asked-one power. We can do worse than ascribe freedom and power to God as we pray for what we want.

· 20 ·

Limited to Everyone

"**N**o salvation outside the church." That phrase has been used over the centuries to express the exclusiveness, or at least the superiority, of Christianity. I have always wondered about it. On the surface, it might seem this phrase is justified, even necessary. There are passages in the Bible which seem to elevate Christ to a position that rules out the validity of all other faiths and orientations. "I am the way, the truth, and the life. No one comes to the Father except by me." So Jesus speaks in the Gospel of John. And there are the great missionary passages urging Christ's followers to go forth and make disciples of every nation. For a good part of its history, the church has seen itself as God's exclusive vehicle for salvation. In the light of this, it has seen its primary task to try to make everybody a Christian. This task has often been carried out from the loftiest of motives. After all, if the only way to God is through Christ, then the highest service we can perform is to bring people to Christ. It all makes marvelous sense in a way, and it stimulated a tremendous effort to take Christianity to every corner of the globe, but I still wonder about it.

No question about it, the Bible is the story of a particular group of people, a single family you could say, and the New Testament is written for a tiny community which is quite distinct from the larger world. But let's look at this a bit. I think we will find that the very specificness of the biblical records leads us away from exclusiveness.

The Hebrews were given their name by the established communities into which they wandered. It meant "drifter." They were nomads living in tents. They were forced to be opportunists, for they lived on the fringes. They were driven to and fro by famine, drought, and political upheaval. They seemed never in charge of their own destiny, always reacting to events, adjusting to changing conditions, making the best of what they found. Yet they managed to survive, even prosper, while other more powerful nations slipped out of history's grip. An early creed began, "A wandering Aramean was my father. . . ." And we hear a psalmist say to the Lord, "I am a stranger with Thee, and a wanderer, as all my fathers were." The "chosen" people of God began as outcasts. They were among the unsettled ones of the ancient Middle East.

From this unsettled existence, the Hebrews sensed God as One on the move. Instead of in great towers, like the Babylonians built for their gods, the Hebrews perceived God's presence in the clouds upon the hilltops. "I lift up mine eyes unto the hills. . . ." Their worship coincided with the movements of their lives and the rhythms of storm, wind, and weather. Their earliest name for God was perhaps El Shaddai, the One of the mountains and storms. And so a conception grew of a God that could not be confined. There was no fixed image that could represent God adequately. "His footsteps move upon the storm," we sing in one of the hymns. This is a God of events rather than places, a God who makes things happen, who leads, listens, speaks, and enters into agreements which later may have to be changed. In the Bible, God deals in the local happenings of a tiny band of nomadic people who live in the backwash of the main history of the Middle East. The biblical God is the leader of a minority group.

Our position in the so-called Christian west may cause us to miss the implications of the biblical situation. We live with the structures of an established Christendom which, though different now than in earlier centuries, are still influential. We don't sense that we are a minority group, but we are. Christianity is not the most adhered to religion in the world. When we take history into account, our minority status becomes even clearer. If the tenure of human beings on earth were reduced to eight hours, the time of the Christian church would be less than a minute. Ours, like that of our Hebrew forebears, is a particular and limited community of faith.

Now, if we let this really sink in for a minute, we are led to a most significant question: How are we to believe that the God of the Bible, the God of this limited, local, Johnny-come-lately tradition, is in fact the God of the universe? How are we to believe that the God of Gods and Lord of Lords, the One almighty, all glorious, all compassionate Deity, is revealed exclusively, or even most clearly, in the lives and events of an insignificant bunch of ragtag wanderers whose homeland has always been a buffer zone between the important powers of that part of the world? And how are we to believe that the Messiah who came from these people is in fact the full and final revelation of God? The answers to these questions do not come from merely quoting a verse or reciting a creed. The answers come as we place ourselves at the disposal of all of our questions about God, as we struggle to affirm whatever faith we have, and as we ponder the implications of our choices.

This is the situation, then. If we say "yes" to the God of the Bible, we become part of a minority group. We take our place with the underdogs of history. We enter a tradition that has always been limited in scope. But we also find that this limited, local minority group has a fantastic understanding of itself. It believes that it exists on behalf of everyone who lives, ever has lived, ever shall live. The promise to Abraham was that his descendents would become a blessing to all the nations. Thus, Abraham's agreement with God reaches far beyond his particular family. And so it is with the Christian church. We say that what God did in Christ is not limited to Christians, but was done for all. The minority group called Israel or church exists for the world. If we take our stand within the specific biblical tradition, we find that its very specificness opens us up to everyone. At its inception, and at its core, this specific tradition was designed to include, embrace, and touch with blessing every life on earth.

Biblical faith does not allow those who believe to think they live in a different world from those who do not believe. Those who believe and those who do not have the same God and Savior. Paul wrote to Timothy, "We work and struggle because we have placed our faith in the living God who is the savior of everyone, especially those who believe." This says, to me, that the specialness of God's people is a representative specialness, not an exclusive one. Those who believe are specific representatives of the general truth which proclaims one God for all. "The sun shines on the evil and the good," Jesus said. Same old sun, same God, same Christ, same world for everybody. Believing doesn't get us privileges, believing is the privilege.

We can't get away from God by not believing in God. We can't avoid God by standing outside the biblical tradition. It is not possible to exist apart from God's gracious activity; it is only possible to be unaware of it or not to care about it. It is possible to live as if God doesn't exist, but that doesn't cause God to cease from existing. All of this was true before Christ came. It is true even if the Christ who comes gets crucified. Nothing stops the one true God. In the way God relates to Christ it is revealed how God relates to all who live and die. The limited biblical tradition through which we perceive these things turns out to be limited to everyone. That is where we end up if we journey very far with the Bible's God.

The salvation of Christ is available to all who live and die. This salvation has been known and received outside the Christian church as well as within it. The purpose of the Incarnation is not to make Christians feel superior; it is to show that God wishes to bless the world through an incarnate, servant people of every stripe, creed, and color. It is to make clear that God is doing just that.

· 21 ·

A Little Dash of Heresy

W hat I have been saying could be criticized for undercutting the missionary and evangelistic activities of the church. I acknowledge the great accomplishments of the missionaries and evangelists, but a lot of that activity has been a very mixed blessing. To my mind, the entire orientation of the enterprise has often been misguided. I realize this may not be a good thing to say in some circles, but I think Christianity and the world it serves would benefit from a closer look at the effort to spread the faith.

I read some years ago about a missionary to Malasia. His task was to work among the Moslems and gather a church. In forty years he only got one convert, and that was his personal servant. He concluded that the idea of getting converts was misplaced, that one aspect of the Christian mission to the Moslems should be to help Moslems become better Moslems, and to learn from Islam how we can be better Christians. Without disparaging the huge missionary effort of the churches over the years, I would say that this man has made a positive contribution to our understanding of what the church's task is worldwide.

Working and writing now in Latin America is one Father Juan Luis Segundo, S.J. His work moves us away from the "them" and "us" mentality that has informed our mission strategy and evangelistic efforts for many years. He points out that in literalistic terms we cannot possibly expect to fulfill the New Testament commission to make disciples of all nations. We have to admit that the vast majority of those who lived and died on earth did so without ever hearing of Jesus Christ. Are we to say they are damned? Or are we to go on with that silliness about how those who don't hear about Christ are pardoned, but those who do hear but don't respond are condemned? That, if we would be kind, is the greatest motivation for not evangelizing I can think of. There has to be another way of going about this.

The church must worship, pray, believe, serve, and give in Christ's name on behalf of all those who don't or won't or can't do these things, and along with all those who do them in other names. This doesn't mean that there won't be differences of opinion over which way may be better. No question, some religious responses are more helpful than others, and I don't see much likelihood of any one big world religion emerging like they dreamed about in the nineteenth century, but neither is it possible any longer to feel that God is triumphant only when everyone becomes Christian. It hasn't happened. It isn't happening. And there is no reason to expect that it will.

We need a new attitude. We need to go with Peter through the experience of the unclean foods. To me, this is the second most important passage in the New Testament. The first is Jesus' prayer in the Garden by which we see that Easter is inevitable. Peter's vision of the unclean foods shows us a struggle we all must go through, and it gives us the clue to its outcome.

Peter was raised a Jew. This meant that he was taught as a boy not to associate with Gentiles. In following Jesus, Peter hadn't gone against anything he held dear. He received Christ's teaching, he followed Christ to the Garden, he shivered in the courtyard of the high priest during the trial, he endured the confusion of the Cross, he marveled at the resurrection. Having gone through all of this, Peter still faced his biggest crisis. He felt, as all the early followers must have felt, that Christ had shown forth God's salvation to the Jews. Surely, they assumed, if Gentiles respond to the gospel, they will take up the practices of the Jewish religion. The Gentile Christians, however, were not about to do this. They were eating what they ate, washing when they washed, worshiping in new ways. To a Jew, such people were ceremonially unclean, all but untouchable.

And there was more to it than ritual. Salvation had come to Peter through the tradition of Abraham, and so it seemed natural that those who were saved would become part of that tradition. To Peter, this was self-evident truth. No salvation outside of Israel. It made all the sense in the world. But then one day Peter had a dream. He saw a picnic of unkosher foods spread before him, and he heard God say, "Come, Peter, rise and eat. What God has cleansed, you must not call unclean." Poor Peter, on top of everything else, he had to go through the shaking experience of being converted right at this point. His decision to follow Jesus was nothing to the upheaval in his soul in regard to his attitude toward Gentiles. Later, at the Gentile Cornelius's house, he says, "I need not tell you that a Jew is forbidden by his religion to visit or associate with a person of another race; yet God has shown me clearly that I must not call any person profane or unclean." In that Gentile company, Peter shows he had changed his long-held inner orientation about what it means to be the people of God.

Peter reveals that we all face two conversions at least. First we struggle with our belief in God and God's salvation, and then we struggle with our attitude toward those who don't take up this struggle in the way we think they should. Faith in Christ, however we come by it, issues in a decision about the relationship between this faith and the rest of the world. "Truly I have perceived," Peter says in his sermon, "that God shows no partiality, but in every nation anyone who fears him and does what is right is acceptable to him." The Word sent to Israel is not an exclusive Word. We need that kind of preaching today. Especially today.

The promise to Abraham is fulfilled in Christ. In Christ we are called upon to complete the opening and widening of our sense of God's blessing. Biblical faith requires us, in each generation, to fight this battle in ourselves and in the wider world. We are not to get boxed in by a great host of biblical texts which speak of a divine exclusiveness. These reflect the popular tradition which prophets and apostles, at their best, tried to correct. Early intimations of these corrections crop up in little dashes of heresy like the story of Jonah and the whale and in the *Book of Ruth*. They say, in effect, "What makes you orthodox believers so sure God's love doesn't go beyond your group? Look what happened to Jonah when he tried to cut off the Ninevites. He got swallowed by a great fish. And look at the Moabitess Ruth. Surely she was more faithful than her Jewish sisters-in-law." The leading edge of the biblical story is always toward the universality of God's love. It bites into the common human tendency toward ruling folks out. It is a painful and necessary bite.

Christ did not come to create a church for believers, he came to reveal a sense of humanity in which mutual love is the reality holding life together. The church exists to know this and show this. The idea of the church universal, says Luis Segundo, is "not rooted in the numerical expansion of a church which is regarded as the exclusive bearer of salvation." That is an exciting sentence. But positively, it says that the universality of the church is rooted in the one true living and loving God who, in a variety of ways in many places, has claimed and saved all of humanity.

What, then, is the role of those who believe? It is to lift up belief, call out belief, show forth the blessedness of belief, share belief, all of this and more, but without the pressure of feeling everyone has to believe. Believers, thus, have an even more important task than promoting belief. Believers are called to believe on behalf of those who don't believe. Scripture, reason, and I hope some common sense, lead me to a position which could be considered heresy, but I see no way to avoid it. God can save people who are not Christians. It happens all the time. It has been going on for ages. The commission to go into all the world and baptize everybody means that everybody's welcome. God can look upon anyone as if he or she were covered with the waters of baptism. God can and does.

· 22 ·

"No Better Thing to Do"

W e have been talking mostly about what we believe in the church and how we can hold to those beliefs amid the struggles of our contemporary lives. It may be time to look at what we do in church. The most important thing we do in church is administer and receive the sacraments.

Sacraments, in the words of the traditional phrase, are "the means of grace." They are events in worship which focus on what God is trying to do all the time. They are rites inside the church which tell of God's presence everywhere. They are the "visible signs of an invisible reality," to paraphrase another definition. They are marks of the church. Based on Old Testament customs to some extent, the Christian sacraments are the communal expression of the church's deepest feelings about itself and its Lord. Protestants celebrate two sacraments, Baptism and the Lord's Supper, and Catholics have seven, including Confirmation, Reconciliation (Penance)—which is tied into the marvelous processes of the Confessional—Ordination of clergy, Matrimony, and the Anointing of the Sick. Both Catholics and Protestants receive sacraments as if they were administered by Christ himself. They are the culmination of Christian worship.

The meanings attached to the sacraments are rich and varied. The water of Baptism can stand for the water of birth, for a kind of death by drowning from which the person emerges reborn, for a cleansing from sin and guilt, and much else. The Lord's Supper commemorates Christ's last meal with his disciples. It is a reenactment of the church's embryonic beginning, a foretaste of the heavenly banquet to come, an expression of love and sharing among the faithful, a seal of remembrance and thanksgiving for Christ's broken body and shed blood. Baptism is once in a lifetime, for God's grace is sufficient from beginning to end. The Lord's Supper is received over and over, acknowledging our need to be constantly renewed and nourished. Sacraments come from the core of the gospel story; they represent events in Christ's life and in our own lives; they bind us together not only in words but in actions; they declare that the community of faith is more than we can perceive or imagine. Someone asked, "Do I kiss because I love, or do I kiss in order to love?" The answer is, of course, both. So it is with sacraments. We celebrate them in order to express our faith, but we also celebrate them in order to have faith, and in order to keep on having faith, day after day and year after year.

Many have said the worship of the church is a drama and the sacraments are its climax. But no play ever had such a run. Dom Gregory Dix has a paragraph in his book *The Shape of the Liturgy* which gives something of the sweep and intensity of observing the Lord's Supper:

> For century after century, spreading slowly to every continent and country and among every race on earth, this action has been done, in every conceivable human circumstance, for every conceivable human need from infancy and before it to extreme old age and after it, from the pinnacles of earthly greatness to the refuge of fugitives in the caves and dens of the earth. Men have found no better thing to do for kings at their crownings and for criminals going to the scaffold; for armies in triumph or for a bride and bridegroom at a little country church; for the proclamation of a dogma or for a good crop of wheat; for the wisdom of the Parliament of a mighty nation or for a sick old woman afraid to die; for a schoolboy sitting in examination or for Columbus setting out to discover America; for the famine of whole provinces or for the soul of

a dead lover; in thankfulness because my father did not die of pneumonia; . . . for the repentence of Margaret; for the settlement of a strike; . . . on the beach at Dunkirk; while the hiss of scythes in the thick June grass came faintly through the windows of the church . . . one could fill many pages with the reasons why men have done this, and not tell a hundredth part of them. And best of all, week by week and month by month, on a hundred thousand successive Sundays, faithfully, unfailingly, across all the parishes of Christendom, the pastors have done this just to *make* the *plebs sancta Dei*—the holy common people of God.

Every time the bread is broken and the cup is shared, it is a different drama, for, since the last time a week ago or three months ago, history has worked itself around to slightly different issues, families are torn by slightly different tensions, whole new sets of covenants have been established or broken. And so worship is always new and the sacraments are always fresh. They seek not only to consolidate those gains already made, but to push beyond them into God's new age.

We can do far worse, if we desire to deepen our faith and touch again our sources, than to think back upon the time we first received Communion, to try to remember the setting, the people there, the sights and sounds and smells surrounding the occasion. Remember how old we were, how we felt, what we wanted, who was important to us. Or, remember other Communions we have received which were especially helpful or meaningful or troubling or happy or sad. Such memories take us to our greatest joys and greatest dangers, to the heights and depths of our lives, and they link us to the life of God. The Communion I remember most vividly is the first one I served as a minister. It was in a Welsh Presbyterian church in Scranton, Pennsylvania, back in 1959. I had made sure I knew the words of the service by heart. I wanted to break the bread and lift the cup while looking into the people's eyes. It almost undid me. After the congregation had sung a ponderous rendition of the Welsh hymn, "Jesus, I live to Thee," I took my place behind the table and lifted the linen covers off the elements. There was a huge hunk of bread which I picked up. I noticed my hands were shaking. I said the words of institution and broke the bread. As I did, I heard something like a gasp from the congregation. I wondered what I had done wrong, but it wasn't that at all. They were just so involved, it meant so much to them, that when I broke the bread it was as if they could feel it inside themselves. Then people bowed their heads and prayed their own prayers while the elders passed the bread up and down the aisles. I had not expected anything like this. I barely made it through the rest of the service and the prayer of thanksgiving. But God knows, I was grateful.

The church can get by without a lot of things, but it can't get by without the sacraments. We need them to secure us to our own histories and to the history of humankind. We need them to make faith real beyond all words and thoughts and prayers and songs. We need them like we need food and drink in order to live, like we need touches and embraces in order to be in love. God knows this. That's why we have sacraments, and that's what makes them holy.

· 23 ·

"In Pictures, Jars
Don't Have to Hold Water"

Some years ago I was teaching English at a nearby college. In those days it was tough going. The students were off to protest the war, join the grape workers strike, and meditate upon their own inner realities. They were also drinking beer, taking drugs, and doing sex, as they called it. I took it as my job to challenge their notion that James Baldwin's *The Fire Next Time* was the greatest piece of literature to find its way into the English language. That I failed miserably is probably to their credit.

As a text for the course I used something called *Theory of Literature* by Wellek and Warren. It is a dull book. The students wouldn't read it. Those were bad days for the theory of anything. But in that text I came across a sentence that has anchored my intellectual life ever since. The sentence was about four types of metaphor used by poets to make connections between apparently unconnected things. "The Lord is my Shepherd," for instance, is a metaphor which identifies God with the caring and watchfulness of a good shepherd. It is a common metaphor throughout the Bible. Wellek and Warren said that the four basic types of metaphoric connection were analogy, double vision, sensuous image revealing the imperceptible, and complete, intense identification. Over the centuries of human speech and literature, these four ways of making meanings have emerged and remained.

Upon reading this, my mind went immediately to my seminary course on the sacraments. Wasn't I told that four basic theories of the Lord's Supper had arisen in the church, each grounded in the history and theology of a particular way of faith? Yes. There is the Roman Catholic theory of "transubstantiation"—the bread and wine are said to become the body and blood of Christ. Then there is Martin Luther's idea of "consubstantiation" in which Christ's body and blood are thought of as present "in, with, and under," the sacramental elements. Calvin taught that while the body and blood of Christ are not locally present in the sacrament, they are spiritually present through images and mysteries which reveal much more than one can see. And finally, there was the Anabaptist position which said that the sacraments were just symbols for the body and blood of Christ, a clearly rational view.

What hits me in this is that the four ways poets use metaphor and the four ways the church has understood the sacraments correspond to each other almost exactly. My feeling is that we are looking at something here which is pretty basic to human communication and basic to our ways of knowing and sensing reality. Santayana said, "Poetry and religion are one." The correspondence between metaphor and sacrament would tend to bear that out. I think poetic metaphor can show us how religious statements and sacraments work, and vice versa. The means of grace and the figures of speech seem to operate in the same four ways.

Let's focus here, though, only on the fourth way of metaphor, that of absolute identity, the one which, to my mind, gets us closest to the deep mystery of divine grace. Modern writers like Kafka and William Carlos Williams are adept at this kind of connection. Things become present in their words. In this kind of writing, the poem does not so much say something with words as mean something through what it is. "The poem creates its own world of virtual reality," says Suzanne Langer, the philosopher of esthetics and poetics. The poem becomes a metaphor of itself, a sacrament of the world it creates. The poem becomes a sacramental universe existing in language. If sacrament depends on Word becoming flesh, then metaphor depends on flesh becoming word. The two processes are that close. Williams' short poem "The Red Wheelbarrow" selects the wheelbarrow, some white chickens, and rain, and it arranges them in sixteen words. It gives a clear, particular perception and no more. If the poem works, it is because it bids us stand in its world, and we do. Something new has been created by the very act of naming it. To me, this is how the fourth kind of metaphor operates, and it is the deepest way we can experience the sacraments. We enter the mode of reality the sacrament creates.

In the Bible we have a mind-set which is compatible with what we have been saying. The Hebrew word for "word" can also mean "thing," "act," "embodiment." In Biblical culture, a word had a life of its own. Things could happen when words were spoken. The words of God were especially potent. "Let there be light," God said. And there was light. In the early centuries it became necessary to state the faith in analytical terms. Mysteries degenerated into problems, and words lost their emotional content and evocative power. For too long, theology has been tied to this kind of language. It is the sacraments rather than the doctrines which have preserved the original unity of God's Word. Sacraments, like metaphors, are possible because thoughts and feelings can be led into imaginative leaps through language. The results of these leaps are identities which otherwise would not exist. These identities can be organized into little poems, great epics, minor myths, and world religions, and, indeed, they have been.

You may suspect that I, a Protestant, am in the position of accepting the Roman Catholic way of the sacraments. You may further suspect that I, who have urged us toward hard thinking, am on the brink of coming out in favor of the least rational approach to the means of grace. If so, you are right. For all the value of rigorous thought, there are times and places when we need to let it go, not forever, not even for very long, but for a brief season while in the presence of such gracious mysteries as the sacraments truly are. When it comes to the sacraments, the attempt to hold on to what is rational is inappropriate. We should not invoke our mysteries too early in theological discussion, lest we have nothing else to say, but when we honestly come upon them, when we are face to face with the Word become flesh, the most radical kind of acceptance of the words as they are spoken is what is called for. "This is my body, broken for you."

Our problem is that we have gotten hung up on a theory of substances—transubstantiation, consubstantiation—rather than look into the nature of language and the way meanings come to be. I hear there have even been chemical analyses done on the sacramental elements in order to prove one thing or another. God help us. Such violence to do to a metaphor. It is unnecessary and uncalled for. For years and years the poets have been using metaphor skillfully and powerfully to bring incongruous things together, creating new realities of thought and word and deed. Metaphors need not be amenable to chemical analysis, though the metaphors of chemists may very well be. One time Picasso was criticized because a jar in one of his paintings didn't look like it could hold water. Picasso's reply was, "In pictures, jars don't have to hold water." Or as Ken Kesey said in the preface to *One Flew Over the Cuckoo's Nest,* "Even if these things didn't happen, they're true."

I am always impressed, when I attend a Roman Catholic Mass, at how the altar boys hold a special dish under the chin of the communicants to catch the wafer, should it fall, or to catch any crumbs which might drop while the wafer is being handled, bitten into, and chewed. I also notice how the priest takes so much care with the chalice, wiping, folding the cloth, wiping again, in an effort to make sure not a particle of what now has become the body and blood of Christ is left to lie casually around the altar. What an appreciation for the thingness of it all. What an expression of the flesh which the Word now has become. What a demonstration of how deeply language can affect us. I believe that if at the most sacred point of the liturgy we hear the words "This is my body, broken for you . . .," then by the grace of God who gives us life and language, we ought to receive that piece of bread as being Christ's body, impossible though it is, irrational though it is, distasteful though it may seem. It is only irrational, impossible, and distasteful if we resist the power and reality of metaphoric speech.

Finally, this fourth mode of metaphor and sacrament rests, more clearly than the others, on the premise that all things are inherently one. Within this mystic oneness there must be a way to grapple with the obvious diversities we experience. There must be room for all the figures of speech to operate. But down deep, when all is said and done, which it never is, there must also be a time and place to set diversity aside in favor of truth's essential oneness. Our view of the sacraments must not prevent that. After all, doesn't the church's preaching also depend on the bringing together of incongruous realities? Do we not say that darkness is really light, sadness really joy, surrender really freedom, weakness really strength, death really life? We can say these things because language allows us to express unities we haven't yet experienced. These unities rest upon, abide in, and gather us to the one true holy and everlasting God. All praise.

· 24 ·

Something Secular

That last was a pretty heady discussion, perhaps too heady and involved, full of the kind of obscurities we ministers are famous for. If so, I'm sorry, but those ideas are important to me. I enjoy opportunities to consider them. One of the good things about being a minister is that we are given time to study, ponder, and reflect. I find a measure of peace and contentment in thinking about spiritual things, and I highly recommend it. But I can't be spiritual all the time. In fact, I can't be spiritual too much of the time. I seem to have a rather low threshold for the tolerance of piety.

Not long ago I went back to Princeton for the twentieth reunion of my seminary class. It was a marvelous time. What a lovely town Princeton is. What a perfect campus for theological study—quiet, orderly, bells ringing every hour calling us to lectures, sermons, hymns, and prayers. We attended two services a day, poked into the various holy places around the quad, had special prayers and messages at meal times, and talked quietly together of church things. When I got home, it was Pentecost. We celebrated three Holy Baptisms and the Lord's Supper. That evening we had a hymn sing. I tell you, I didn't want to be in church that night. All the goodness and truth I could absorb for a while had already been absorbed. I had reached the limit of my capacity to benefit from holy occasions. I needed something secular.

I longed to look at an old Humphrey Bogart movie. I felt

famished for ordinary music ordinarily played. I wanted to read the magazine section or the funny papers and consider nothing more earth-shaking than the advertures of Alley Oop. I probably shouldn't be telling you this, but if your faith depends on thinking preachers and their ilk are always happiest when they are preaching, praying, singing hymns and thinking tall thoughts, you're in trouble anyway. I can stand only so much of that kind of thing before I get to hankering for the sights and sounds and stories of the secular world. It's just the way it is. I can no more pray without ceasing than keep my desk clean, and I haven't had a clean desk in years.

I notice that when I become overchurched, my soul starts to rebel. My mind grabs hold of whatever distraction lies at hand. My spirit begins to chuckle in a devilish way at the minor misfortunes of others. I just performed a wedding, and there was a lady there, as there often is, who was very important. Somehow, she was in charge. She got us through the service all right and then took over the reception. She was dressed in a most lavish, tight-fitting powder-blue pantsuit, and she had, without knowing it, backed into the stove and gotten a huge ugly grease spot right on her bottom. I probably shouldn't have been looking at that, but I was beginning to find it just short of hilarious. She was making everything perfect all around her, directing this one here and that one there, and yet when she turned around, there it was—grease and dirt calling attention to the limits of our ability to have everything perfect.

I have a weakness for the ordinary, nonreligious things of this world. After a week of church and the spiritual quest, my heart cries out for the Rotary Club, the stock market, or some good old-fashioned cussing over a missed putt. To be too long in the religious realm is like being too long with your relatives. It's good to see them and it's good to see them go. I get so I need to look at grimy streets and the writing on unholy walls. I receive something from the rush and screech of traffic that I can't get from a hymn. I am hopelessly bound up with this world.

We went to see *Ain't Misbehavin'*, the revue based on the career of Fats Waller. There's a song in it about a reefer five-feet-long sung and danced by a fellow who is supposed to be higher than a kite. My preacher soul, I suppose, should have been shocked. I should have taken notes, so I could use that song as an excuse to condemn all sorts of things. But the truth is, I enjoyed it. The guy was great. The whole evening was great. There are times when my philosophy of life corresponds to that of Louis Armstrong's when he said, "I'm not tryin' to prove nothin', I'm just tryin' to see a good show."

I don't know how this fits in with the command to love God with all my heart, mind, soul, and strength, even though I believe that Jesus gives one of the keys to life in that commandment. I like to sing the gospel song "Do Lord," which talks about this world not being my home, "I'm just a'passing through," but I know darn well there is much in this world that fascinates me and gives me pleasure. I have heard that we are supposed to be "in the world, but not of it," but I've never quite gotten hold of how to do that. I am *of* the world, and I love it.

I take comfort in an understanding of biblical faith as incarnational, worldly, in touch with matter as well as spirit. After all, Jesus' favorite name for himself was "Son of Man." A better rendering of that phrase for our time might be Herman Waetjen's "the Human Being." At the heart of all we know about God is the Human Being. That is vintage Christianity. And there is tucked away in the Old Testament the *Book of Ecclesiastes,* which calls everything vain and doesn't much mention God. It pleases me no end that right there in the Bible is a book about life and the world from a purely secular point of view that has for its subtitle, "The Preacher." Apparently the sheer force of its writing and worldly wisdom earned it a place among the sacred texts. And there is that marvelous perspective of the psalmist, "Lord, you have searched me and known me. . . ." Somehow, God knows what it's like for me to be who I am in this world. God knows, and God accepts, and there are moments when I know God loves me in my down-to-earth secular self. There is nothing more secular than a cross, and there is nothing more sacred either. Perhaps we should let go of the sacred/secular distinction. God is one. The creation is good. Nothing exists or happens which is not charged with the possibility of a visit from God. I'm going to worry less and less about my penchant for something secular. It's the least I can do.

· 25 ·

Hymns

I stand with Lewis Thomas, president of Memorial Sloan Ketter-
ing Cancer Institute in New York, when he says that music is
the best thing we humans do. In fact I told that to Charlie Mussel-
white, a Chicago blues singer, and he said, "Oh no, makin' babies
is the best thing humans do."

"The way you sing," I told him, "I'm not sure there's much
difference, and anyway, where does the basic beat come from?" He
only grinned.

Lewis Thomas, who is beautifully optimistic about the human
enterprise, says, "Any species capable of producing, at this earliest
juvenile stage of its development . . . the music of Johann Sebastian
Bach, cannot be all bad." I agree. Apparently others agree too. If
I'm not mistaken, when they sent the space capsule out to make
contact with other forms of life, they included a recording and the
score of Bach's "Jesu, Thou Joy of Man's Desiring." I have to say
that's putting our best foot forward on many fronts. I am more than
happy to be so represented in the worlds and galaxies beyond us.

Music may be the best thing we do in church too. Faith has
inspired some of humanity's finest sounds. Every great movement
among the peoples and nations of earth has had its songs. Singing
does something that nothing else can do to pull us together, give
us courage, express our sorrows and our hopes. When it comes to
praising God, sooner or later we must break into singing. Lectures,
discussions, teachings, rituals, and all the rest just aren't enough.

I like all kinds of music, and all kinds of church music, except maybe the thump-thump-thump of rock n' roll. I like the classical anthems, the gospel songs, the spirituals. It is a source of satisfaction to me that the church has been right at the heart of the musical tradition of the western world. "Secular" music is a Johnny-come-lately. I'm not sure there is anything secular about music anyway. Luther took beer-hall tunes and made them into hymns. Were those songs "the devil's music," as he put it, before he borrowed them for the church? No. The absence of specific religious content does not make a song un-Godly.

My favorite church music is the singing of the people. The two places where this has moved me the most are in the Welsh congregations I've known and in the black churches I've visited. These people know something about singing that the rest of us need to learn. It may be that they have a higher percentage of gifted voices in their churches than we do, but I don't think so. I think they sound the way they do because their singing comes from their own history and experience and from a deep sense of the unity between life and God. The music wells up inside them and gives utterance to all the pain, uncertainty, and glory they feel.

In those Welsh churches of northeastern Pennsylvania where I started out as a preacher, they still have "Gymanfa Ganus," Welsh hymn sings with the congregations and choirs of many churches getting together for an afternoon and evening of song. At the front of the church, on these occasions, there is usually a harp to go along with the organ and piano which are always there. The hymns are ponderous, often written in minor keys, moving slowly and with steady purpose. The Welsh are in no hurry to get through a song. "We are living, we are dwelling, in a grand and awful time," a famous one begins in its English version. "Once to every man and nation comes the moment to decide," begins another. They are well-written, highly structured hymns, full of the pressures of living. One must almost frown to sing them properly. The lips of the people at a Welsh hymn sing often form little scallops in a row, the corners of their mouths pointing down. There are lively ones too:

"LLanfair" for instance, to which we sing "Praise the Lord his glories show, Alleluia." For seriousness, depth, and dedication to a musical tradition, Welsh hymn singing cannot be surpassed.

On my very first Sunday in the Welsh congregation in Scranton, I happened to choose "Cwm Rhondda" for the final hymn. We know it as "Guide me, O Thou Great Jehovah." I chose it because it is a stirring hymn, a prayer to God for guidance and deliverance through the uncharted stretches of life, a good attitude with which to begin a pastorate I thought. That choice was one of the best I ever made as a minister. I had no idea then that "Cwm Rhondda" is a sort of Welsh national anthem. I didn't realize that I was only the second pastor of that church who didn't speak and preach in Welsh, a truly impossible language. The people consider it the language of the angels, and it may very well be, for all I could learn of it. That my name was Jones, and that I had chosen "Cwm Rhondda" for the final hymn that day, saved me.

We got to the end of the hymn and the people were singing the chorus at the top of their lungs, "Songs of praises, Songs of praises, I will ever give to Thee, I will ever give to Thee." I had never heard anything like it. Presbyterians singing like that! The Choirmaster, who in a Welsh church is just a little lower than God, waved his arm in a huge arc over my head, and the people went back to the first chorus. "Bread of heaven, Bread of heaven, Feed me till I want no more, Feed me till I want no more." They closed their eyes, they shut their hymn books, they threw back their heads, they broke into parts, and really began to sing. There were few more than a hundred there, but the effect was that of a throng. And it wasn't just volume, it was feeling, attitude, tone. Tears streamed down faces as the people sang and sang the chorus of that hymn. I had never dreamed that a church service could be so ringing, so powerful. I shared their faith, their common history, their joys and pains, even though I didn't know them at all. And I felt the authenticity of their expression. I learned more about being a pastor in that moment than I had learned up to that time. I learned that the church is not so much what we preachers say it is, but what the people sing about and pray for. Everywhere I've gone I have recognized something of what those people in Scranton showed me that day.

A clue to the power of Welsh hymn singing may come from the stories I heard in Scranton about what happened in the days when the coal mines were working full bore, and there was an explosion or cave-in down below. A whistle would sound and the people would gather to find out who was trapped. Volunteers stepped forth to begin a rescue, for it was an unwritten code among miners that no one, dead or alive, was left underground. Then the church bells would ring, calling the people to prayer and song. If many of the old Welsh hymns seem to come out of the bowels of the earth, this may be why. They are the aching tones, slow rhythms, deep, haunting words and syllables of sung prayers for those in darkness and danger. These services went on and on. Late in the night the lights of the church would be turned off so that the worshipers might identify with their trapped loved ones in the caverns beneath them. Then a single candle would be lit and placed on the communion table, and the people would begin to sing the hymn "Sandon," which in English goes like this:

> *Lead, kindly Light, amid the encircling*
> *gloom,*
> *Lead thou me on;*
> *The night is dark, and I am far from home;*
> *Lead thou me on!*
> *Keep thou my feet; I do not wish to see*
> *The distant scene: one step enough for me.*

How about that for getting down to it in worship. And it's not only the Welsh or the blacks who know how to reach into God's heart through a hymn. It happens in all congregations, and it brings forth great power and devotion. I have heard it happen.

· 26 ·

The Last Word

Christianity, perhaps more than any of the religions, is a faith for the end of the age. There is evidence that the New Testament writers were as much concerned with how everything was going to turn out as with anything else. Their writings leave us with vivid descriptions of the culmination of all things. Some of these descriptions are scary, others are terribly obscure. And some of the passages about last things would seem to contradict what we have been saying about God's inclusiveness. There is that sheep and goats business, for instance, which can sound as if eventually some are in and some are out. Let's see if we can find our way through these difficulties to a wholesome view of this significant part of Christian faith.

In the New Testament we have several pictures of the end of the age. New Testament studies are now done with an eye to what the first believers thought was going to happen when everything was over. Some of those believers looked for the end in their lifetimes. They thought Jesus would come back, set things right, and peace would reign. Some of them even stopped working and decided to wait around for the end to come. It didn't. Paul told them to get back to work or else forget about eating. Their timing was obviously way off. The things they were waiting for haven't happened yet, and so we find it necessary to think about what to do if the world doesn't end. In a way, it's easier to decide what to do if you know the world is ending than if you don't. But we don't know. "No one knows the hour or the day," Jesus said.

Jesus gave us two kinds of stories about what the end of the world might be like. He spoke, as we said, about sheep and goats, wheat and tares, some kind of division between the righteous and the unrighteous. There is paradise and there is the burning pit. This, I suppose, is the dominant image people have of what the Bible says about these things. It's enough to make one tremble. But we also have a different kind of story. Feasts and parties and weddings are given as pictures of the way God will wind things up. An interesting feature of some of these parties is the business of the guest list. It often has little resemblance to the people who actually attend the feast. In these stories, it is impossible to tell ahead of time who is in and who is out. To me, these stories indicate the new, gospel insight into the matter of the final things. God is more inclusive than we think, they seem to say. Along with those passages about a great division and the traditional scenes of gnashing teeth, there are texts that tell of a final victory for God in which none is lost, no, not one. We are free to decide which texts are in control. I hope by now you don't have to ask how I come out on that decision. God wins. That's the message of the wedding feast and banquet passages. It's the message of the *Book of Revelation*. I like to think God really wins. That means no one and nothing is lost.

But just as the Bible doesn't tell us everything about the beginning of things, so it doesn't tell us everything about the end. We know now, as they did not know in Bible times, that our earthly home is but a small sphere near a rather unimpressive star at the tip of a whirl in a galaxy we have quaintly named The Milky Way. We know that the number of galaxies like ours is uncountable. We know that a single galaxy can contain billions of stars more significant than our sun. And so any picture we make of the end of the earth has to take its place in the midst of all that complexity of spinning light. Furthermore, the principles by which all of this seems to live and move are barely known. Therefore, to claim, on the basis of some Bible verses, that we know the details of the ultimate future of all things is utterly preposterous. The Bible was never meant to be used like that.

However, it is possible to have a picture of the ultimate goal of all things which is not inconsistent with the Bible and which, at the same time, does not fly in the face of what is presently known. All of "nature and history are knit together toward a divinely intended goal," is the way one theologian puts it. God not only creates, not only pushes existence out of the nest so to speak, God also receives it all back. God receives it back however it comes, changed however it is changed, for better or for worse. And so God is affected by what happens. The movements of history, the processes of nature, the decisions of men and women, the flukes and accidents, can cause God joy or pain. The life, death, and resurrection of Jesus Christ is for Christians a demonstration of God's involvement in all of this. Christ shows us God's heart and face. The Lord of the universe bleeds over what can happen. And Christ shows us God's unflinching steps toward the next event, the next moment, the next experience. With Christ, we move toward surprising occasions in which the worst situations can bring forth victories. The final event, however it is conceived, is a triumph of God.

God's goal is the widest possible sharing of love. God desires the fullest actualizing of every potential. And God lures us and all creation toward that goal. God attracts. There is a pull between us and the Almighty One like the pull between us and those we love. All things, all events, all persons, live and move in what might be called an erotic whole that draws reality together. In the Greek language *eros,* from which our word "erotic" comes, means much more than something sleazy. It means life force, creative impulse, consummation. It is one of the Greek words for "love." It could very well be that *eros* makes the world go round, as the old song says.

God, we have tried to say, is the chief creative force in the universe. And so God is the primary and final effect of all the movements of creation. If we take into account all the worlds of which we are aware—and we must take them into account or our

God is not really God at all—then it is hard to say more than what we have said. The processes of creation seem to go on. If there is a completion in one place, there is a beginning someplace else. A dying star here, a new source of light there. A time may come when everything ends, but it doesn't seem likely, given what we know of the magnitude of what's out there. And anyway, we don't really know enough to say. It is possible that our solar system is running down, but even if it is, there are still a huge number of other solar systems going about the business of being and becoming. God is not defeated even by what would be for us total defeat. We have a Cross at the core of history to show us that.

Yet, we are not left with a mere attempt to attach our significance to the significance of what outlasts us. We don't need to ride toward meaning on the coattails of the galaxies. God is the ultimate recipient of everything that happens. The falling sparrow somehow registers as does the falling star. Everything is kept. What we accomplish is collected and preserved in the very being and moving of God. I am sure this is what we express at the graveside when we commit a person's body to the ground. "Blessed are the dead from henceforth; yea says the Spirit, that they may rest from their labors, and their works do follow them." A more contemporary expression is "God takes unto himself and treasures the occasions one by one." How it all turns out matters to God, and so God does everything that can be done to keep it from turning out badly. By the very nature of who God is, our times, our deeds, our lives, are kept safe.

The Bible begins with a picture of God at work creating the world. The Bible ends with a benediction and an "Amen." In between is a story which takes our breath away if we let it. The sweep and majesty of every human struggle and glory is included. Then there is that final and fitting "Amen." We usually translate the word "So be it." That's not good enough. In Hebrew, "amen" refers to what is reliable, firm, true, securely founded, proven, ready, and loyal. When we use the word at the end of a prayer it means we give our assent to the praise or petition being offered to God. To say "Amen" is to put ourselves into the foregoing statements in all earnestness and enthusiasm. It is to secure ourselves in the phrases of a prayer. In the prophecy of Isaiah we have the term "the God of amen," and in *Revelation*, Jesus is called "the amen." Amen is the last word, a sure word, a word of completion, fulfillment, hope. It is, ultimately, God's word, a name for God. God has the last word. The last word is God.

· 27 ·

Not Etched in Stone

I hope it is clear that there are many ways to hold to basic beliefs. I hope I have shown that Christianity allows for this kind of diversity, even though churches can seem pretty rigid sometimes. And I hope I have given a sense of the way important beliefs can change and develop and still be all right. We are not stuck with what they told us in Sunday school forever. Life will not allow us to live by what we believed as children. We will be stretched by our occasions, and our faith must stretch too, or we will lose it. A set of beliefs doesn't have to be etched in stone in order to be valid. In fact, once beliefs get etched in stone they are usually out of date. Life goes on. God moves. Our thoughts must change.

Rather than beliefs we are stuck with, I would like us to have affirmations we can live by. Affirmations can expand and grow. They can be pruned and changed. As we finish this up, I'll give you a few affirmations I like to take with me.

I am a child of God. God made me with the same care as God created the universe. God gave me all I need for happiness, wisdom, and faith.

My life has purpose and meaning. I am part of God's plan for creation. My personal history is woven into the histories of the lives around me, and together we take our places in the long story of God's activity which begins and ends in God's love.

The sufferings and disappointments of my life are not final. The

Cross of Christ shows me that God is affected by all that is wrong as well as by all that is right. The same power which brought Christ from the grave is at work in me. Nothing holds me in one place forever. I move, in all my experiences, closer and closer to my true end in God.

I am loved. The cosmic, unbounded love of God comes to me in a personal way. "Jesus loves me this I know, for the Bible tells me so." I affirm that and live by it. God always turns out to be more merciful than I have believed or expected. This mercy I receive from God can give me the capacity and desire to be merciful. When I act upon that desire, I am most happy.

God hears my prayers. God knows what I want before I ask. God knows my troubles before I tell them. In the telling, I take a step toward deeper communication with God. As I look into my life, I find the answers to my prayers.

God claims me for life eternal. Fears and uncertainties need not cloud my thoughts about the future. Nothing I do or say, nothing in all creation, cuts me off from God in any final way. Even on that day when the earth claims my body and I return to the dust, I am answering a divine call. Praise be to the living God.

We all have affirmations. They need not be ponderous or grand. They need not be permanent or binding. They need not be like anybody else's. And they need not sound like the official language of the church. But it helps to express one's sense of place in the universe, one's deep feelings for life and people, one's values and important hopes. It helps to have our own words to look at from time to time to see where we are with our inner selves. It helps to draw up one's courage, and in the midst of all that is troubling and threatening to us, say some positive things. Thus, I list my affirmations. I invite you to list yours.